LF

A Handbook of Structured Experiences for Human Relations Training

Volume VII

Edited by

J. WILLIAM PFEIFFER, Ph.D.

JOHN E. JONES, Ph.D.

UNIVERSITY ASSOCIATES
8517 Production Avenue
P.O. Box 26240
San Diego, California 92126

SERIES IN HUMAN RELATIONS TRAINING

PREFACE

As we write this preface, it is two years since the last volume of *A Handbook of Structured Experiences for Human Relations Training* was published. We are concerned that no volume be dominated by variations of previously published structured experiences. Variations do, however, serve an important function: they allow the facilitator to continue to use "tried and true" favorites while avoiding the boredom and sense of mechanical repetition that accompanies overuse of one or a few structured experiences.

It appears to us that more structured experiences are being developed than ever before, as the use of structured experiences for training and learning has become legitimate and even common. When we initiated this series, we had a huge backlog of uncataloged structured experiences. The first four volumes of *A Handbook of Structured Experiences for Human Relations Training* organized and made available these extensive resources. The volumes published since then (V, VI, and VII) and the Structured Experiences sections of *The Annual Handbooks for Group Facilitators* draw almost exclusively on newly created experiences.

This volume, like most of its predecessors, contains two dozen structured experiences, most of them original. Users are encouraged to adapt and modify them to suit their own unique needs and circumstances. In producing this volume, we have tried to make the designs as generally applicable as possible, avoiding those suited only to relatively specialized uses.

As with all University Associates publications, users may freely reproduce these materials for educational or training purposes. *For large-scale distribution or the inclusion of materials in publications for sale, prior written permission is required.*

We at University Associates continue to hold the professional value that resources should be shared by peers. The *Handbooks of Structured Experiences for Human Relations Training* are one important evidence of this belief. We continue to invite users to participate in this process, through feedback suggestions and by sending us materials that have proven helpful for them.

We are very grateful to many people who have helped make this volume of the *Handbook* possible, among them, Beverly A. Gaw, who served as content consultant, and Arlette Ballew, staff editor, whose endless patience with details deserves a special note of recognition.

J. William Pfeiffer
John E. Jones

La Jolla, California
December, 1978

iii

TABLE OF CONTENTS

---

*See Introduction, p. 3, for explanation of numbering.

INTRODUCTION

Our early work in creating learning designs led us to the use of what had always been termed "exercises," "techniques," or "games." When we made the decision to gather these valuable materials into a book, we became concerned that "exercise" and "game" had connotations we considered dysfunctional to the intent of their use. We therefore elected to call them "structured experiences," to indicate that they are designed for experience-based learning.

Our interest in providing participants with a distinctive design for human relations training has resulted in an increasing orientation in our consulting activities, laboratories, and workshops toward experiences that produce generally predictable outcomes. In designing human relations training experiences, we strive to become aware of and to examine the specific needs of the client system or particular group and then develop learning situations that will meet those needs. Based on an experiential model, structured experiences are inductive rather than deductive, providing *direct* rather than vicarious learnings. Thus, participants *discover* meaning for themselves and *validate* their own experience.

A variety of experiential learning models have been developed in recent years (see Kolb & Fry, 1975; Kolb, Rubin, & McIntyre, 1971). Our own version has five steps that occur in a cycle:

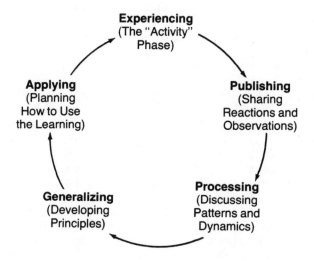

The *experiencing* phase involves some activity such as fantasy, dyadic sharing, or group problem solving. If the model stopped at this point, however, training would be only "fun and games." Next, the participants engage in *publishing* their reactions to and observations of the activity. This is the data-generation

1

phase; it leads logically into *processing*. It is our belief that processing is the key to the potency of structured experiences, and it is important that the facilitator allow sufficient time for this step. If the training is to transfer to the "real world," it is important for the participants to be able to extrapolate the experience from a laboratory setting to the outside world through *generalizing*. In this phase, participants develop principles, hypotheses, and generalizations that can be discussed in the final phase, *applying*. This final phase must not be left to chance; facilitators need to ensure that participants recognize the relevance of the learning. The actual application of behavior becomes a new experience and begins the cycle again.

There is no successful way to cut short this cycle. If structured experiences are to be effective, the facilitator must supply adequate opportunities for "talk-through." The payoff comes when the participants learn *useful* things that they take responsibility for applying.

Thus, a concern that we bring to all our training publications is the need for adequate processing of the training experience so that participants are able to integrate the learning without the stress generated by unresolved feelings about the experience. It is at this point that the expertise of the facilitator becomes crucial if the experience is to be responsive to the learning and emotional needs of the participants. The facilitator must judge whether he or she will be able successfully to process the data that probably will emerge in the group through the structured experience. Any facilitator, regardless of background, who is committed to the growth of individuals in the group can usefully employ structured experiences. The choice of a particular activity must be made using two criteria: the facilitator's competence and the participants' needs.

As in the previous volumes of the *Handbook*, the sequencing of structured experiences in Volume VII has been based on the amount of understanding, skill, and experience needed by the facilitator to use each experience effectively. The first structured experience, therefore, requires much less background on the part of the facilitator than does the last. The earlier experiences generate less affect and less data than do those near the end of the book, and, consequently, the facilitator needs less skill in processing to use them effectively and responsibly.

It is also the responsibility of the facilitator to examine the specific needs and the level of sophistication of the group and to choose a suitable structured experience. Adaptability and flexibility are therefore emphasized in the design of the structured experiences in this volume. The variations listed after each structured experience suggest possible alterations that a facilitator may wish to incorporate in order to make the experience more suitable to the particular design and to the needs of the participants. The expected norm in human relations training is innovation.

Our use of and experimentation with structured experiences led us to an interest in developing useful, uncomplicated questionnaires, opinionnaires, and other instruments. It is our belief that instruments enhance and reinforce the learning from structured experiences. Instruments also provide feedback to the facilitator on the appropriateness of the activity and the effectiveness of the presentation.

Some instruments appeared in the first volumes of these *Handbooks* and have subsequently been revised and refined in later editions. Each volume of the *Handbooks* contains structured experiences that include instruments. We find that the complementary selection of structured experiences and instruments can create powerful learning environments for participants, and we encourage those involved in the field of human relations training to become acquainted with this twofold approach in providing for participants' learning needs.

At the end of each structured experience in this volume are cross references to similar structured experiences, suggested instruments, and lecturette sources that seem especially appropriate to that experience. The number of each supplemental or complementary structured experience and the publication in which it appears are indicated. Instruments and lecturettes are listed by title and publication. Space for notes on each structured experience has been provided for the convenience of the facilitator.

Our published structured experiences are numbered consecutively throughout the series of *Handbooks* and *Annuals*, in order of publication of the volumes. A list of all structured experiences by category is found at the end of this book. (This list also appears in the 1979 *Annual*.) Although this categorization is somewhat arbitrary, since any experience may be adapted for a variety of uses, it will aid the facilitator in choosing an appropriate activity.

The contents of the entire series of *Handbooks* and *Annuals* are fully indexed in the new *Reference Guide to Handbooks and Annuals* (3rd ed). The *Reference Guide* is an indispensable aid in locating a particular structured experience or a structured experience for a particular purpose, as well as related instruments, lecturettes, and theory articles.

The purpose, then, of the *Handbooks* is to share further the training materials that we have found to be useful in training designs. Some of the experiences that appear here originated within University Associates, and some were submitted to us by facilitators in the field. It is gratifying to find that facilitators around the world are using the *Handbooks* and concur with our philosophy that sharing these valuable materials with others is far more in the spirit of human relations theory than the stagnating concept of "ownership" of ideas.

Users are encouraged to submit structured experiences, instruments they have developed, and papers they have written that might be of interest to practitioners in human relations training. In this manner, our Series in Human Relations Training will continue to serve as a clearinghouse for ideas developed by group facilitators.

REFERENCES

Kolb, D. A., & Fry R. Toward an applied theory of experiential learning. In C. L. Cooper (Ed.), *Theories of group processes*. New York: John Wiley, 1975.

Kolb, D. A., Rubin, I. M., & McIntyre, J. M. *Organizational psychology: An experiential approach*. Englewood Cliffs, NJ: Prentice-Hall, 1971.

245. TEA PARTY: AN ICE BREAKER

Goals

    I. To allow participants to share experiences and perceptions in a nonthreatening manner.

    II. To promote acquaintance and a feeling of interaction in a new group.

Group Size

    Four to eighteen members.

Time Required

    Fifteen minutes to one hour.

Materials

    One Tea Party Booklet for each member. (The booklet should be prepared in such a way that participants are presented statements one at a time.)

Physical Setting

    Enough room for participants to move around and converse freely in two lines, facing each other.

Process

    I. The facilitator introduces the activity as an opportunity for members to get to know one another in a fanciful way. He reminds them of the scene in *Alice in Wonderland* in which Alice came upon a tea party attended by the Mad Hatter, the Dormouse (who seemed to be asleep most of the time), and the March Hare. They spent the time telling each other stories, and when they had used their dishes, instead of washing them, they simply moved around the table to clean places. The facilitator tells the participants that they have been invited to just such a tea party.

    II. The facilitator instructs the participants to arrange themselves standing in two lines facing each other, with a comfortable distance between them, as though they were seated across a long table. If there is an odd number of members, one member takes the position at "the head of the table."

Even number	Odd number	
x x x x x x	x x x x x	
x x x x x x	x x x x x	x

III. The facilitator distributes a Tea Party Booklet to each member. He tells them that the activity consists of a series of paired conversations. Each pair will share one topic (one page of the booklet) for at least two minutes. Then each member will move one place to the left, turn the page, and share the next topic with a new partner. The activity will continue until each member has shared with every other member.

IV. The facilitator explains that since the Dormouse is asleep during most of the tea party and may be trampled in the shuffle, one person must "sit" with him during each round. If there is an *even* number of members, one member will volunteer to remain with the imaginary Dormouse while the rest of the members rotate. This person will share in the dialog with whoever is across from him. If there is an *odd* number of group members, all members rotate, but the person at the head of the table during each round—the "Dormouse sitter"—will not have a partner for that round (this person may keep time for the round).

V. The facilitator tells the members to open their books to page 1 and to begin the first round of sharing. He (or the odd-numbered Dormouse sitter) calls time for each round and instructs the members to move on to the next partner and the next topic for sharing.

VI. When all members have shared with each other, the facilitator assembles the group and leads a discussion of the experience. He may focus on such discussion items as:
1. Was it easy or difficult to share the topics? ("on a scale of one to ten . . .")
2. What happened during the sharing process?
3. What were your feelings *during* the activity and *about* the experience?
4. What did you learn from the experience?
5. How can these learnings be applied in the group and in other situations?

VII. If the group has an odd number of members, they can be asked to comment on what they observed during their inactive rounds as "Dormouse sitters."

Variations

I. If there are fewer than eighteen members, participants can be instructed either to continue rotating until the booklet is completed or to pair off with their last "new" partner in the cycle and continue the sharing process in dyads.

II. The booklet can be used exclusively in dyads, without the tea-party structure.

III. The content of the booklet can be edited to fit the purposes of the group.

Similar Structured Experiences: *Vol. I:* Structured Experience 5; *Vol. II:* **25**; *Vol. III:* **49, 70**; *Vol. IV:* **101, 123.**

Suggested Instruments: *Vol. IV:* "Risk-Taking Behavior in Groups Questionnaire"; *'74 Annual:* "Self-Disclosure Questionnaire."

Lecturette Sources: *'73 Annual:* "The Johari Window: A Model for Soliciting and Giving Feedback," "Conditions Which Hinder Effective Communication," "Risk Taking"; *'74 Annual:* "Five Components Contributing to Effective Interpersonal Communications."

Notes on the Use of "Tea Party":

Submitted by Don Keyworth.

TEA PARTY BOOKLET

The facilitator should prepare a booklet for each participant. The booklet should be assembled so that only one page can be read at a time.

TEA PARTY: AN ICE BREAKER   1

Instructions: With each new partner, turn to a new page in this booklet   2
and take turns sharing the topic printed there. Do not skip pages. Do not
look ahead in this booklet.

One of my favorite times of the year is . . .   3

A pleasant memory from my childhood is associated with . . .   4

Quickly choose one of the following or fill in your own subject: 5

The first time I:

    tried to swim, I . . .
    was away from home overnight, I . . .
    kissed someone outside the family, I . . .
    performed before a group, I . . .
    went out on a real "date," I . . .

A person whom I would like to visit is . . .   6

One of my favorite spots to spend some time is . . .   7

(Continue)

If I could take you there right now, I . . .

If I could change my vocation (job), I would . . .   8

Paraphrase your partner's response: "What I hear you saying is . . ."

I am eagerly looking forward to (something anytime in the future) . . .   9

Look over the past pages and pick one topic you would like to return to and share that with this partner.   10

Pick one: 11

    When I first got together with the chief significant-other person in my life right now (spouse, lover, good friend, etc.), I . . .

    What I remember most about my closest childhood friend is . . .

When I can find some time to be alone, I like to . . .   12

Give your partner some "impressions" as feedback: "You seem to be a person who . . ."

I came to this session because . . .   13
(If time permits) So far during this tea party I have felt . . .

Three things that I think I am really good at are . . .   14

One thing about me that I would like to change is . . .   15

Share with your partner a personal success that you have experienced   16
and what it means to you.

A problem that I am dealing with right now is . . .   17

Pick a topic from the last pages and ask your partner to tell you his   18
or her answer to it.

Now that we have reached the last page in this booklet, I feel . . .   19

---

246. PERSONAL IDENTITY: AN ICE BREAKER

Goals

I. To enable participants to "try on" new identities.

II. To explore the influence of a different identity on the behavior of others.

III. To explore the relationship between honesty and trust.

Group Size

Eight to twenty-four participants in two to four groups of four to six persons each. (Most members should not know each other.)

Time Required

Approximately one hour.

Materials

I. A copy each of version A of the Personal Identity Instruction Sheet for half the participants.

II. A copy each of version B of the Personal Identity Instruction Sheet for the other half of the participants.

Physical Setting

A room large enough for the groups to meet without interfering with or being overheard by each other. If more than one room is used, it should be possible for the facilitator to visit each group during the time the participants are getting to know each other.

Process

I. The facilitator tells the group members that an important part of the time they spend together will be getting to know each other personally and that to facilitate this he will divide them into smaller groups. He tells them to avoid being in a group in which there are other persons they already know. If this is unavoidable, they are to behave as though they do not know anyone in the group.

11

II. Groups are formed, and the facilitator distributes a copy of the Personal Identity Instruction Sheet to each member. The number of persons receiving form A in the group should approximately equal the number of persons receiving form B in the group.

III. Participants are directed to read the Personal Identity Instruction Sheet. They are told that they have approximately twenty minutes to get to know each other, that they may begin by having each person in succession take two minutes to tell about himself, and that they may comment on any presentation after all are completed.

IV. The facilitator calls time and announces a fifteen-minute break during which participants are free to leave the room if they wish. They are encouraged to continue the process of getting to know other members of their group. This step is important in order to give them an opportunity to interact on the basis of their presented identities, whether genuine or false.

V. The entire group is reassembled, and the facilitator asks the members to identify any other members whom they believe to have presented false identities. When all the "nominations" have been made, those members who have assumed different identities identify themselves.

VI. The facilitator leads a discussion of the experience. He may include such questions as:
1. What are the feelings of those who presented themselves honestly about those whom they suspected of presenting a made-up identity? Were they tempted to embellish their own presentations?
2. Did those with "false" instructions assume that others also were lying?
3. Did this influence their behavior?
4. Did any members find that people related to their new identity differently from the way people usually relate to them?
5. Will it be hard for those who were told false stories to get to know or to trust the "false" persons in the future?
6. Did members find it easy or difficult to "lie"?
7. What did each member learn about himself from this?
8. Is it necessary or important that people be honest about themselves? Are there any virtues in not being honest about oneself?

Variations

I. The information that some members are presenting different identities can be withheld until Step V.

II. Every member can be instructed to assume a new identity.

III. Members can be given the choice of either presenting a true identity or trying a new one.

IV. Members can divide into groups of "old" and "new" identities after the break to discuss their experiences before reporting to the entire group.

Similar Structured Experiences: *Vol. I:* Structured Experience 1; *Vol. II:* **42**; *Vol. III:* **49**; *'76 Annual:* **174, 180, 182;** *Vol. VI:* **198.**

Suggested Instruments: *Vol. III:* "Intentions and Choices Inventory"; *'74 Annual:* "Self-Disclosure Questionnaire"; *Vol. IV:* "Risk-Taking Behavior in Groups Questionnaire."

Lecturette Sources: *'72 Annual:* "Defense Mechanisms in Groups," "Communication Modes: An Experiential Lecture," "Openness, Collusion and Feedback"; *'73 Annual:* "The Johari Window: A Model for Soliciting and Giving Feedback," "Risk-Taking"; *'75 Annual:* "Human Needs and Behavior"; *'76 Annual:* "Clarity of Expression in Interpersonal Communication."

Notes on the Use of "Personal Identity":

Submitted by David E. Whiteside.

PERSONAL IDENTITY INSTRUCTION SHEET   A

In order for group members to get acquainted with each other, each member is first to talk briefly about himself or herself to the group for approximately two minutes. After each person has done this, other members are free to comment on whatever anyone spoke about. For example, you might want to question someone about an experience he has had or relate it to your own experience. Remember, the goals are to obtain information about the other persons in the group and to supply information about yourself. What you initially tell the group about yourself can be basic information such as birthplace, occupation, interests, etc., or it can be more idiosyncratic, such as astrological sign, favorite color, shoe size, favorite fantasy, etc. In short, you can tell the group members anything that you think will help them to get to know you. You will have fifteen minutes to get to know each other. Then you may take a break, during which time you will continue to interact informally with members of your group.

Some members of the group will be presenting false pictures of themselves. You may wish to see if you can identify whether a member's story is true or false, but do not "cross-examine" another member solely for this purpose. The atmosphere in the group is to remain one of getting acquainted. If you know that another member is presenting a false picture of himself, do not reveal this to anyone.

Do not share these instructions with anyone.

PERSONAL IDENTITY INSTRUCTION SHEET   B

In order for group members to get acquainted with each other, each member is first to talk briefly about himself or herself to the group for approximately two minutes. After each person has done this, you may attempt to find out more about the people in the group and they about you. Your task, however, is to *not* tell the truth about yourself. Keep your real name, but make up a new identity for yourself that is entirely or largely false. Thus, you can talk about such things as birthplace, occupation, interests, etc., or about more idiosyncratic things such as astrological sign, favorite color, shoe size, favorite fantasy, etc., but what you say should be false or highly misleading. Try to make your story or your "facts" believable and consistent. (After this activity, the group will take a short break. Continue to maintain your "new" identity during this period as you interact informally with the members of your group.)

Not all people will be receiving these instructions. It is crucial that you do not indicate in any fashion that you are not telling the truth or that you have received these instructions. Try to see how well you can act. If you find yourself in a group with someone who also is presenting a different identity, do not reveal this to anyone.

Do not share these instructions.

247. PREJUDICE: AN AWARENESS-EXPANSION ACTIVITY

Goals

I. To share feelings and ideas about prejudices in a nonthreatening manner.

II. To explore the validity of common prejudices.

Group Size

An unlimited number of groups of three members each.

Time Required

One to one and one-half hours.

Materials

I. Two blank 3″ x 5″ index cards for each participant.

II. Ten 3″ x 5″ index cards prepared ahead of time according to the Directions for Preparing Prejudice Cards.

III. A pencil for each participant.

Physical Setting

For each group, a grouping of three chairs arranged in a triangle, with one chair facing the other two.

Process

I. The facilitator distributes two blank index cards and a pencil to each participant. He reads the list of ten prejudices from the prepared cards and directs the participants to write one additional object of prejudice on each of their two blank cards, a different item on each card.

II. The facilitator collects the index cards, adds them to the ten prepared cards, and shuffles the stack.

III. The facilitator divides the participants into triads. One member from each group takes two cards off the top of the stack, looks at both and selects one. The other card is returned to the stack. Each of these members then returns to his place, facing the other two members of the triad.

IV. The member with the card in each triad announces the subject of his card to his group. The other group members verbally assault and make disparaging or stereotyped remarks about the subject of prejudice, while the member holding the card refutes their statements and defends the item or group being attacked. (Three to five minutes.)

V. Each member takes a turn being the person who selects a card and defends the object of prejudice.

VI. The facilitator leads the total group in a discussion of the following points:
1. What types of prejudicial statements were made by the participants?
2. Did any participants admit having any prejudices? What were they?
3. Were any prejudices held in common by a number of members?
4. How did the selected members defend the objects of the prejudices?
5. How did the members feel when they were seated alone defending their subject against the other group members?
6. How did members feel if they perceived themselves as fitting a stereotyped subject?
7. How did members feel when they were making stereotypical remarks?
8. What did this experience tell group members about their own prejudicial perceptions and behavior?

The facilitator then leads a discussion of the fallacies of the usual prejudices found in society today, the results of such attitudes, and ways to deal with or refute them.

Variations

I. The experience can be conducted in dyads.

II. The stereotype can be role played.

III. The stereotype can be defended by a person who is a member of the stereotyped group.

IV. Participants can be asked to defend a subject against which they are personally prejudiced.

V. Each participant can choose any card to defend.

Similar Structured Experiences: *Vol. III:* Structured Experiences **62, 63;** *'73 Annual:* **95;** *Vol. IV:* **112;** *Vol. VI:* **203, 213, 215, 217;** *Vol. VII:* **258, 262, 267.**

Suggested Instruments: *'72 Annual:* "Supervisory Attitudes: The X-Y Scale"; *'73 Annual:* "Sex-Role Stereotyping Rating Scale"; *'77 Annual:* "Bem Sex-Role Inventory (BSRI)."

Lecturette Sources: *'72 Annual:* "Assumptions About the Nature of Man"; *'75 Annual:* "Nonverbal Communication and the Intercultural Encounter"; *'76 Annual:* "Making Judgments Descriptive"; *'79 Annual:* "Anybody with Eyes Can See the Facts!"

Notes on the Use of "Prejudice":

Submitted by Richard Raine.

DIRECTIONS FOR PREPARING PREJUDICE CARDS

On *each* of *ten* 3″ x 5″ index cards, write the name of *one* thing or group that is commonly the object of prejudice.

Sample Items

Women	Catholics
Blacks	Jews
Foreigners	WASPs
Italians	Redheads
Polish people	Fat people
Mexicans	Drinkers
Arabs	Smokers
Police	Loud people
Bureaucracy	Neon colors
Politicians	Hard-rock music
Old people	Motorcycles
Children	Gun advocates
Spiders	Intellectuals
Homosexuals	Southerners
Military	Hillbillies
Academicians	Hippies
Asians	Car salesmen
Big cities	Dog or cat owners
Small towns	Socialites
Democrats	Republicans

248. ALPHA II: CLARIFYING SEXUAL VALUES

Goals

   I. To explore attitudes regarding sexual mores.

   II. To compare sexual values with others.

   III. To practice group consensus seeking.

Group Size

     An unlimited number of groups of four members each (preferably two males and two females).

Time Required

     Two to two and one-half hours.

Materials

   I. An Alpha II Suggested Regulations Sheet for each participant.

   II. An Alpha II Consensus Evaluation Sheet for each participant.

   III. A pencil for each participant.

   IV. Newsprint and a felt-tipped marker for each group and for the facilitator.

   V. Masking tape.

Process

   I. The facilitator distributes a copy of the Alpha II Suggested Regulations Sheet and a pencil to each group member and allows a few minutes for all to read the material. He then directs each member to select or revise five rules from the list that should be included and to note any rules that should be excluded from the regulations. The following guidelines may be considered in compiling a list of regulations:
     1. What patterns of sexual behavior do I require of myself?
     2. What rules of sexual conduct am I willing to let others have?

   II. The participants take ten to fifteen minutes to compile their lists.

III. The facilitator calls time. He forms groups of (preferably) two males and two females each and announces that each group's task is to submit a consensus report of the rules that each group thinks are the most important rules to be considered by the entire colony. He says that the newsprint may be used to compile the group's list and that the following guidelines are to be followed in reaching a group decision:

1. No averaging, majority rule, or trading is to be used to reach group consensus.
2. There must be *substantial agreement* on any given rule before it is considered accepted.
3. The opinions of the more quiet group members should be solicited.
4. The group's task must be completed in one hour.

IV. At the end of fifty-five minutes, the facilitator gives a five-minute warning. At the appropriate time, he stops the group activity and asks for the consensus list of regulations from each group. He posts the groups' lists and discusses them in terms of:

1. What is similar on the groups' lists? What is different?
2. What is conspicuously missing on the lists? Why were these items or issues not dealt with?
3. Which rules "look good on paper" but might be difficult in practice?
4. What do these lists suggest about the total group as a community? How does that fit with the larger environment?
5. How might these rules be put to good use in the members' own behavior?

V. The facilitator distributes the Alpha II Consensus Evaluation Sheet to all members and allows them five minutes to rank the listed items individually.

VI. At the end of that time, he leads a group discussion of the experience. He may include the following questions:

1. How did your values and beliefs affect your decision making? The group's decision making?
2. What are some personally significant learnings from this experience?
3. How might this experience affect our understanding of larger social issues, e.g., ERA, gay rights?

Variations

I. Separate groups of males and females can be formed and their lists compared and contrasted.

II. Strongly felt minority reports can be allowed.

III. The groups can be the "International Control Commission" instead of a recommendation committee.

IV. Rules can be generated for other issues such as politics or religion.

V. The total group can compile and rank items in one list.

Similar Structured Experiences: *Vol. I:* Structured Experience **15;** *Vol. III:* **62, 63;** *'73 Annual:* **94, 95;** *'76 Annual:* **184;** *Vol. VI:* **215;** *'78 Annual:* **226;** *Vol. VII:* **249, 258, 268.**

Suggested Instruments: *Vol. III:* "Polarization: Opinionnaire on Womanhood"; *'73 Annual:* "Sex-Role Stereotyping Rating Scale"; *'77 Annual:* "Bem Sex-Role Inventory (BSRI)"; *'79 Annual:* "Women as Managers Scale (WAMS)."

Lecturette Source: *'77 Annual:* "Androgyny."

Notes on the Use of "Alpha II":

Submitted by Don Keyworth.

ALPHA II SUGGESTED REGULATIONS SHEET

Background: Scientists have discovered that the second planet orbiting Alpha Centauri is almost an exact duplicate of earth, except there are no intelligent life forms. A colonization party, including you and your group, has been formed to settle on Alpha II. The five hundred members of the colonization party come from many different countries and cultures with many differing customs and mores.

Instructions: Your group has been asked to recommend a list of the five most important rules from the list below to govern sexual conduct and relationships both on the space journey and on Alpha II. You need not concern yourself with questions of enforcement—assume that all rules can be enforced.

Rules Recommended by the International Control Commission (to be revised):

1. A couple may have a child only after being certified as meeting specified minimum psychological and physical requirements.
2. Any form of sexual activity between consenting adults is allowed.
3. There shall be no marriages as such, but any two or more adults may certify their intention to live together.
4. Individuals intending to live together shall first sign a contract specifying the terms of ownership for their possessions and finances.
5. Any individuals participating in sadomasochistic activities shall be subject to punishment by the colony.
6. Both males and females shall practice effective birth-control methods.
7. Any unapproved pregnancy shall be aborted.
8. Approved pregnancies that are no longer desired can be aborted only with the consent of the colony council.
9. Any newborn infant judged to be sufficiently deformed or retarded as to be incapable of maturing to normal adult self-sufficiency shall be put to death painlessly.
10. There shall be no public display of sexual behavior, but sexually explicit literature and films will be available privately as desired.
11. No individual shall be discriminated against because of his or her sexual preferences.
12. Each individual shall participate regularly in both private and group counseling on sexual attitudes and behavior.
13. Consistent with future population needs, selected couples shall be offered special incentives to bear children.

ALPHA II CONSENSUS EVALUATION SHEET

Instructions: Rank the items below by circling the appropriate number from 1 (very little) to 5 (very much) that indicates how you felt about the group-consensus activity that you have just completed.

1. I felt frustrated during the group activity.   1   2   3   4   5

2. I felt that I was "listened to" by the other group members.   1   2   3   4   5

3. I think my values were acknowledged by the other group members.   1   2   3   4   5

4. I actively sought contributions from others.   1   2   3   4   5

5. I agreed with the group's final report.   1   2   3   4   5

6. The group members were supportive and accepting of each other, even during disagreements.   1   2   3   4   5

7. This activity was personally significant to me.   1   2   3   4   5

8. I learned something about my personal sexual beliefs and values.   1   2   3   4   5

249. SEXUAL VALUES: RELATIONSHIP CLARIFICATION

Goals

    I. To identify one's own values about a sexual relationship.

    II. To become aware of the sexual values of others.

    III. To increase awareness of the many components of sexual relationships.

Group Size

Unlimited.

Time Required

One and one-half hours.

Materials

    I. A copy of the Sexual Values Work Sheet for each participant.

    II. A pencil for each participant.

    III. Ten posters (large sheets of paper or newsprint), on each of which is written a different number from 0 to 9, and masking tape.

    IV. Newsprint and a felt-tipped marker.

Physical Setting

A writing surface for each participant.

Process

    I. The facilitator solicits from the group a list of positive and negative factors or qualities (values) inherent in a sexual relationship. He writes these on newsprint and then identifies the most common ones.

    II. The facilitator distributes a copy of the Sexual Values Work Sheet and a pencil to each participant. He says that each participant is to write a number—any number: telephone, house, social security, student identification, drivers' license, waist size—in the upper right corner of the work sheet and to remember the number. He then tells the participants to read

24

the directions on the Sexual Values Work Sheet and to add any elements or values from the newsprint list that they wish to those on the work sheet.

III. Each member of the group takes about fifteen minutes to fill out the Sexual Values Work Sheet.

IV. The facilitator calls time, collects the work sheets, and redistributes them at random to the participants so that no person ends up with his or her own work sheet.

V. The facilitator tells the participants that they are to provide feedback on the work sheets they received. He instructs them to use the data on the work sheets they have been given and to write as objectively as possible (a) what they think is important to this person in a sexual relationship; (b) what might interfere with this person's sexual relationships; and (c) any first impressions they have about this person as a result of the work sheet. Any blank space on the front and back of the Sexual Values Work Sheet can be used for these responses. He tells the participants to sign their names on the work sheets to indicate the source of the feedback. (Fifteen to twenty minutes.)

VI. While the participants are completing the feedback, the facilitator places the posters with the numbers 0-9 around the room, spacing them to accommodate the size of the group.

VII. Participants are instructed to place the work sheets they have just evaluated in front of the appropriate numerical designation according to the last digit of the identification number placed on the work sheet by the participant who originally filled it out. For example, if the original identification number is 2004873, the work sheet is put in the place designated for threes.

VIII. When all work sheets are placed, each participant retrieves his or her own work sheet from the stacks. Participants take five minutes to read the feedback. The participants then mill around as each finds the source of his feedback in order to clarify and react to what he read.

IX. The facilitator leads a discussion of the experience, focusing on the following aspects:
1. Feelings of the participants about receiving feedback;
2. Feelings about the task of filling out the work sheet;
3. Feelings about giving others feedback about their sexual values;
4. Common results or inferences resulting from the experience (for example, what values seemed to emerge as necessary to a good sexual relationship or hindering a satisfactory sexual relationship? Were certain impressions correlated with certain values?);

5. New insights on the part of participants about their own or others' sexual values and the influence those have on present relationships. How might the participants behave differently in or about sexual relationships as a result of these new insights?

Variation

Participants can rank a limited set of dimensions on the work sheet from the most important to the least important. The facilitator sums up the value listed for each dimension and divides by the total number of participants to discover the average ranking for each dimension. This information is discussed by the group. Separate tabulations can be done by persons of different ages, sexes, etc., in order to examine the differences.

Similar Structured Experiences: *'73 Annual:* Structured Experiences **93, 94, 95;** *'75 Annual:* **143;** *'76 Annual:* **184;** *'78 Annual:* **226;** *Vol. VII:* **248, 258, 268.**

Suggested Instruments: *'73 Annual:* "Sex-Role Stereotyping Rating Scale," "Scale of Feelings and Behavior of Love"; *'74 Annual:* "Self-Disclosure Questionnaire"; *'75 Annual:* "Scale of Marriage Problems"; *'77 Annual:* "Bem Sex-Role Inventory (BSRI)."

Lecturette Sources: *'73 Annual:* "Risk Taking," "Dependency and Intimacy," "Some Implications of Value Clarification for Organization Development"; *'75 Annual:* "Giving Feedback: An Interpersonal Skill"; *'76 Annual:* "Interpersonal Feedback as Consensual Validation of Constructs"; *'77 Annual:* "Androgyny."

Notes on the Use of "Sexual Values":

Submitted by Paul S. Weikert.

SEXUAL VALUES WORK SHEET

Each of us has certain criteria, standards, and values for entering into and sustaining a relationship that involves sexuality. The following is a list of values that are sometimes involved in sexual relationships.

There are some factors that you want to be *present* in your sexual relationship. You are to select the five most important of these and rank them from one to five ("1" is most important, "5" is least important). You may add any values from the group's list that you think should be added and use them in your rankings.

There are some factors that you would want to be *absent* in your sexual relationship. Select five of these and also rank them from one to five (the *least* desirable factor being "1"). You also may want to use some of the negative factors on the group's list.

1. Age	16. Possessiveness
2. Attraction	17. Race or ethnicity
3. Commitment	18. Reciprocity
4. Companionship	19. Religion
5. Consideration	20. Respect
6. Contraceptive protection	21. Security
7. Dependence	22. Third-party involvement
8. Equality	23. Trust
9. Expectations	24. Experimentation
10. Feeling at ease	25. Pressure
11. Honesty	26. Dominance
12. Interdependence	27. Communication
13. Jealousy	28. Variety
14. Love	29. Frequency
15. Openness	30. Security

250. MEANINGS ARE IN PEOPLE: PERCEPTION CHECKING

Goals

I. To demonstrate that meanings are not in words but in the people who use them and hear them.

II. To illustrate that our perceptions of words attribute positive, neutral, and negative meanings to them.

Group Size

Up to ten groups of four to six members each.

Time Required

One to three hours.

Materials

I. A copy of the Meanings Are in People Work Sheet for each participant.

II. A copy of the Meanings Are in People Group Summary Sheet for each group.

III. A pencil for each participant.

IV. Newsprint and a felt-tipped marker for each group.

Physical Setting

A table for each group or other writing surfaces for participants.

Process

I. The facilitator forms small groups of four to six members each and distributes a copy of the Meanings Are in People Work Sheet and a pencil to each participant and a copy of the Meanings Are in People Group Summary Sheet to each group.

II. The facilitator assigns each group a different word from one set of the Meanings Are in People Target Words and directs members to write their group's word on their copies of the Meanings Are in People Work Sheet.

III. The facilitator directs that each person independently is to list on the Meanings Are in People Work Sheet all the words that come to his mind when he thinks about the assigned target word.

IV. After five minutes, the facilitator directs participants to assign a positive (+), neutral (O), or negative (−) value to each word they listed.

V. Steps II, III, and IV are repeated up to five times, each time with different target words assigned to each group.

VI. Each member of each group totals the number of positive, negative, or neutral values for each of the assigned group words in the space provided on the Meanings Are in People Work Sheet.

VII. Group members then identify associated words that were listed more than once by members of the group for each assigned word and list them on the Meanings Are in People Group Summary Sheet. They indicate how many positive, negative, and neutral values were assigned to each common word. Each group then copies its summary on newsprint. For example:

Assigned Target Word	Common Words Associated with Target Word	Value		
		+	−	O
Women's Liberation				
	1. Equality	4		2
	2. Social Movement	3	2	2
	3. Radical	1	2	

VIII. The facilitator collects the groups' newsprint summaries, posts them, and reassembles the total group. He then discusses the number of positive, negative, or neutral words associated with each assigned target word and notes the words identified more than once.

IX. The facilitator leads a discussion of the experience, including:
1. How the different values associated with words illustrate that their meanings are in the people who use them, not in the words;
2. How our perceptions of words affect our communication effectiveness (including examples of this principle);
3. What individual participants learned from the experience about themselves and their own use of words;
4. How members plan to apply these learnings in the future.

Structured Experience 250

Variations

I. Locally controversial topic words can be chosen as target words.

II. More group interaction can be stimulated by discussing all the associated words in the total group rather than reporting only repeated ones.

III. All groups can be assigned the same target word in each round.

IV. A combination of "objective" and "loaded" target words can be given and the different reactions compared and contrasted.

V. Members can be instructed to assign positive, neutral, or negative values to the assigned target words first, before they develop and label the associated words.

Similar Structured Experiences: *Vol. II:* Structured Experiences **28, 42;** *Vol. III:* **63;** *'73 Annual:* **91, 94, 95;** *Vol. V:* **168;** *'76 Annual:* **174, 180;** *Vol. VI:* **217;** *'78 Annual:* **227;** *'79 Annual:* **241;** *Vol. VII:* **247.**

Suggested Instruments: *'74 Annual:* "Interpersonal Communication Inventory," "Self-Disclosure Questionnaire."

Lecturette Sources: *'73 Annual:* "Conditions Which Hinder Effective Communication"; *'74 Annual:* "Five Components Contributing to Effective Interpersonal Communications"; *'76 Annual:* "Clarity of Expression in Interpersonal Communication"; *'78 Annual:* "Communication Effectiveness: Active Listening and Sending Feeling Messages," "Communicating Communication."

Notes on the Use of "Meanings Are in People":

Submitted by Jack N. Wismer.

MEANINGS ARE IN PEOPLE TARGET WORDS

Instructions to the facilitator: These words are arranged in sets *horizontally.* Select a set and assign a different target word from it to each group, duplicating the words if there are more than five groups.

milk	coffee	tea	alcohol	water
Republican	Democrat	communism	socialist	democracy
rural	city	town	country	home
rules	freedom	instructions	procedures	regulations
wildflower	tree	weed	flower	leaf
chicken	vegetables	ice cream	salad	sugar
parent	child	relationship	affair	relatives
pride	emotion	independent	assertive	feeling
ice	hard	hot	cold	soft
boss	manager	employee	supervisor	subordinate
ocean	lake	river	desert	stream
animal	chick	seagull	bird	dogs
woman	chauvinist	nurse	girls	housewife
fireman	army	policeman	cop	soldier
civil servant	politician	bureaucracy	election	liberal
learning	experience	college	school	education
job	profession	task	vacation	duty
freeway	traffic	automobile	road	lane
tradition	conventional	unusual	fancy	plain
evaluation	appraisal	interview	support	discussion
details	involvement	complication	decisions	puzzle
arithmetic	math	study	files	calculation
foreign	adventure	sophisticated	risk	shy

MEANINGS ARE IN PEOPLE WORK SHEET

Assigned Target Word	Common Words Associated with Target Word	Value + − O
	1. 2. 3. 4. 5. 6.	
	1. 2. 3. 4. 5. 6.	
	1. 2. 3. 4. 5. 6.	
	1. 2. 3. 4. 5. 6.	
	1. 2. 3. 4. 5. 6.	
		Total

MEANINGS ARE IN PEOPLE GROUP SUMMARY SHEET

Assigned Target Word	Common Words Associated with Target Word	Value + − ○
	1. 2. 3. 4. 5. 6.	
	1. 2. 3. 4. 5. 6.	
	1. 2. 3. 4. 5. 6.	
	1. 2. 3. 4. 5. 6.	

Total

251. MIXED MESSAGES: A COMMUNICATION EXPERIMENT

Goals

   I. To explore the dynamics of receiving verbal and nonverbal communication cues that are in conflict with one another.

   II. To examine how nonverbal cues can convey listener attitudes that can affect the communication process.

   III. To develop an understanding of the importance and impact of being direct and congruent in all forms of interpersonal communication.

Group Size

     A minimum of four triads is most effective. (One or two extra members can join triads to serve as additional process observers.)

Time Required

     Approximately forty-five minutes to one hour.

Materials

   I. A copy of the Mixed Messages Communicator Instruction Sheet for one member of each triad.

   II. A copy of the Mixed Messages Observer Instruction Sheet and a pencil for the second member in each triad.

   III. One of four different Mixed Messages Listener Instruction Sheets ("Anything You Can Do, I Can Do Better," "Who Gives a Damn," "How Sweet It Is," or "This Is How It Ought To Be") for the third member in each triad. If there are more than four triads, one or more listener roles can be duplicated.

   IV. Newsprint and a felt-tipped marker (optional).

Physical Setting

     Enough room for the triads to work without disturbing each other. The observer in each triad should be seated slightly away from the communicator and listener.

Process

I. The facilitator divides the group into triads, disperses them about the room, and tells them to talk about whatever they wish.

II. After five minutes, the facilitator gives a copy of the Mixed Messages Communicator Instruction Sheet to one member of each triad, a copy of the Mixed Messages Observer Instruction Sheet and a pencil to another member of each triad, and a copy of one of the four Mixed Messages Listener Instruction Sheets to the remaining member of each triad. Members are told only that one person in each triad is a communicator, one a listener, and one an observer.

III. Participants are then told to read their instruction sheets, but not to discuss the information on them with other members. When all members have read their instruction sheets, the facilitator tells them to begin the activity.

IV. After ten minutes, the facilitator stops the communicator/listener phase and instructs the members to share their role instructions. Observers are told to report their observations (to give feedback) to communicators and listeners.

V. After ten minutes of observer reports, the large group reassembles for a discussion of the effects the different listener roles had on the feelings and perceptions of the communicators. The facilitator briefly explains each listener role, and members discuss:
1. How it felt to play the different listener roles;
2. How it felt to try to communicate with the different types of listeners (including frustrations and satisfactions);
3. The level of communication achieved by each triad and each type of listener.
The facilitator may list or chart major points on newsprint.

VI. The facilitator examines and develops the importance of congruence, clarity, and openness in communication, at both verbal and nonverbal levels. He then solicits comments from participants on how these learnings can best be applied in their various back-home situations.

Variations

I. The facilitator can direct the members of each triad to exchange cards with another triad after the observer report in order to give members an opportunity to try out new roles.

II. Observers can become communicators, communicators listeners, and listeners observers in the second round.

Structured Experience   251

III. There can be four rounds, with all groups simultaneously using the same listener role and a different role being used during each round.

IV. If there is only one round, each listener role can be demonstrated to the total group before the discussion phase.

Similar Structured Experiences: *Vol. I:* Structured Experience **8**; *Vol. III:* **50, 52**; *Vol. V:* **152, 153**; *'76 Annual:* **183**; *Vol. VII:* **252.**

Suggested Instruments: *'72 Annual:* "Interpersonal Relationship Rating Scale"; *'74 Annual:* "Interpersonal Communication Inventory."

Lecturette Sources: *'73 Annual:* "Conditions Which Hinder Effective Communication"; *'74 Annual:* "Five Components Contributing to Effective Interpersonal Communication," "'Don't You Think that . . .?': An Experiential Lecture on Indirect and Direct Communication"; *'76 Annual:* "Clarity of Expression in Interpersonal Communications"; *'78 Annual:* "Communication Effectiveness: Active Listening and Sending Feeling Messages," "Communicating Communication."

Notes on the Use of "Mixed Messages":

Submitted by Branton K. Holmberg and Daniel W. Mullene.

MIXED MESSAGES COMMUNICATOR INSTRUCTION SHEET

You and your listener are simply to carry on the conversation that your triad has already started. Try your best to communicate your message to your partner. It is your responsibility to keep the conversation going. Do not discuss or share these instructions at this time.

MIXED MESSAGES OBSERVER INSTRUCTION SHEET

Your task is simply to collect data on what the communicator and listener are doing during their conversation. Do not concern yourself with the *content* of the conversation, but write down your observations about the *processes* they are using to communicate. Pay attention to what the listener and communicator do (eye contact, gestures, body positions, and other nonverbal behavior).

Describe what you observe as accurately as possible without judging it. You will be asked later to give feedback to the communicator and listener. Do not discuss or share these instructions at this time.

MIXED MESSAGES LISTENER INSTRUCTION SHEET

"Anything You Can Do, I Can Do Better"
You and your communicator are to continue the conversation that your triad started a few minutes ago. You are to appear attentive and to listen carefully to your partner, but you are to challenge everything your partner says. You may interrupt while he or she is talking, anticipate what would have been said next, and disagree or present your own point of view. You may point your finger, lean forward as if about to pounce, and engage in other nonverbal behaviors that accent your verbal behavior. You are the critic.

After you have made your criticism or statement, wait and allow your partner to begin the conversation again. Your task is *not* to take over the conversation but merely to interrupt, disagree, or challenge whatever is said. If your partner hesitates, remain silent until he or she begins to talk again, and then resume your role. Do not discuss or share these instructions at this time.

Structured Experience   251

MIXED MESSAGES LISTENER INSTRUCTION SHEET

"Who Gives a Damn?"

You and your communicator are to continue the conversation that your triad started a few minutes ago. You are to listen carefully to what your partner is saying, but are to send your partner nonverbal signals that indicate your boredom (i.e., look away, doodle, slump in your chair or sprawl on the floor, twist and fidget, clean your fingernails, fiddle with your clothing, or such). If your partner accuses you of being uninterested, insist that you are interested—you may even review what has been said—but continue to send nonverbal signs of boredom. Do not discuss or share these instructions at this time.

MIXED MESSAGES LISTENER INSTRUCTION SHEET

"How Sweet It Is"

You and your communicator are to continue the conversation that your triad started a few minutes ago. You are to appear attentive, listen carefully, and agree with everything your partner says, regardless of your own opinions on the subject. When your real opinion is opposite of what your partner is saying, smile as you indicate agreement. You may make comments such as "That's a good (great) way of putting that," "That's very insightful of you," "Oh, wow," and so on. Resist any invitation from your partner to share your ideas ("Oh, I agree with you") or to criticize or evaluate the ideas being communicated. Do not discuss or share these instructions at this time.

MIXED MESSAGES LISTENER INSTRUCTION SHEET

"This Is How It Ought To Be"

You and your communicator are to continue the conversation that your triad started a few minutes ago. You are to listen carefully to your partner and actively pursue the ideas your partner is sharing with you. Indicate that you understand his or her ideas by paraphrasing (restating) them. If you disagree, simply state your ideas calmly and logically. Ask for clarification or examples if these would be helpful. You also can indicate that you are interested in the conversation by the use of nonverbal cues such as establishing eye contact and leaning toward the speaker. Do not attempt to lead the conversation or change its direction. Although your partner is the "communicator," you are to play an active part in making the communication process as clear and mutual as possible. Do not discuss or share these instructions at this time.

252. ACTIVE LISTENING: A COMMUNICATION-SKILLS PRACTICE

Goals

 I. To identify the emotional messages that are often hidden in communication.

 II. To gain practice in active-listening skills.

Group Size

An unlimited number of dyads.

Time Required

Approximately one and one-half hours.

Materials

 I. Two copies of the Active Listening Work Sheet for each participant.

 II. A copy of the Active Listening Feedback Sheet for each participant.

 III. A pencil for each participant.

Physical Setting

An area in which the dyads can talk without disturbing each other.

Process

 I. The facilitator gives a lecturette on active-listening skills. He emphasizes that people communicate much more than words or ideas and that strong feelings often lie behind the words. He points out the confusion that often results from the difference between "think" and "feel " and the nonverbal cues that can reveal feelings that are not verbalized.

 II. The facilitator divides the group into dyads (pairs) and directs that each of them is to identify one member as the employee and the other as the supervisor.

 III. The facilitator gives a copy of the Active Listening Work Sheet and a pencil to each participant. He goes over the instructions and tells the participants that they will have twenty minutes in which to complete the activity.

IV. After twenty minutes, the facilitator calls time. He distributes a second copy of the Active Listening Work Sheet to each participant and directs the participants to reverse roles and repeat the activity with different members playing the supervisor and the employee.

V. After twenty minutes, the facilitator calls time and reassembles the total group. He gives each participant a copy of the Active Listening Feedback Sheet. He goes over the suggested responses with the participants. Any questions are discussed by the group. (Ten to fifteen minutes.)

VI. The facilitator directs each dyad to write on the back of the Active Listening Feedback Sheet one or more observations about the experience and conclusions about how active-listening skills can help or hinder effective communication. (Five minutes.)

VII. The observations and reactions of members are shared. The facilitator then leads a discussion on the application of active-listening skills.

Variations

I. Situations and messages can be developed to suit the needs of the group (e.g., parent-child, teacher-student, husband-wife, counselor-client, etc.).

II. The activity can be done individually, and responses compared with a partner.

III. The activity can be done as a group effort, with the group composing the active-listening responses.

IV. The activity can be set up so that only the person giving the message sees the script. The listener responds as in a role play.

Similar Structured Experiences: *Vol. I:* Structured Experience 8; *Vol. III:* **50, 52, 65;** *Vol. V:* **152;** *76 Annual:* **183;** *Vol. VII:* **250, 251.**

Suggested Instruments: *'72 Annual:* "Interpersonal Relationship Rating Scale"; *'73 Annual:* "Helping Relationships Inventory"; *'74 Annual:* "Interpersonal Communication Inventory."

Lecturette Sources: *'72 Annual:* "Communication Modes: An Experiential Lecture"; *'73 Annual:* "Conditions Which Hinder Effective Communication," "Thinking and Feeling"; *'74 Annual:* "Five Components Contributing to Effective Interpersonal Communications"; *'76 Annual:* "Clarity of Expression in Interpersonal Communication"; *'78 Annual:* "Communication Effectiveness: Active Listening and Sending Feeling Messages," "Communicating Communication."

Submitted by Jack N. Wismer.

Notes on the Use of "Active Listening":

ACTIVE LISTENING WORK SHEET

Instructions: People communicate much more than words or ideas. Behind the words often lie feelings. These *feelings* often are communicated through nonverbal means, even while conflicting *ideas* are communicated verbally. Trying to look and listen for feelings, write an active-listening response for each situation and message on this sheet.

The employee will begin by reading Statement 1, and the supervisor will give an active-listening response. The supervisor will then read Statement 2, and the employee will give an active-listening response. This process will continue, with the employee reading all odd-numbered statements and the supervisor reading all even-numbered statements.

As each member gives a response, it should be noted in the space provided.

Example

Situation and Message:	*Active-Listening Response:*
Supervisor sets policy that he or she will sign all letters. Employee says: "I want to sign my own letters. I wrote them, didn't I?"	The supervisor responds: "You feel frustrated (resentful) when you are not allowed to sign letters that you have written."

Situation and Message:	*Active-Listening Response:*
1. Supervisor says a report is not thorough enough. Employee says: "Now I have to write this report over. You never tell me what you expect until it is written."	1. The supervisor responds:
2. Supervisor must meet a report deadline. Supervisor says: "We have got to be better organized."	2. The employee responds:
3. Employee is not implementing supervisor's ideas. Employee says: "I was on this job long before you came here. I don't need you to tell me how to do it."	3. The supervisor responds:

Situation and Message:	*Active-Listening Response:*
4. Regular staff meeting never starts on time. Supervisor says: "I get tired of waiting for some people every week before we can start these meetings."	4. The employee responds:
5. Supervisor has just made a project-team assignment. Employee says: "I don't want to work with Bill on any more assignments. He never meets his deadlines."	5. The supervisor responds:
6. An employee has not turned in the last two monthly progress reports. Supervisor says: "Can't you be as professional as the rest of the staff and turn in your report on time?"	6. The employee responds:
7. Supervisor has initiated a new work procedure. Employee says: "We tried something like this three years ago and it didn't work then."	7. The supervisor responds:
8. Supervisor recognizes that some employees' talk is so loud it is interfering with other employees' writing a report. Supervisor says: "Can't you be more considerate while others are trying to work?"	8. The employee responds:

Situation and Message:	*Active-Listening Response:*
9. Supervisor has passed on a change in work priorities from the top office. Employee says: "You give us too much unscheduled work. I never can get it all done."	9. The supervisor responds:
10. Employee has refused to work overtime on a project. Supervisor says: "Young people today are lazy!"	10. The employee responds:

ACTIVE LISTENING FEEDBACK SHEET

This sheet provides some possible responses for each situation; it is not intended to identify "correct" responses. A response may well be influenced by the way in which you perceive the situation and the intonation that accompanies the verbal message you receive. In some of these situations, the speaker appears to be more defensive than in others. If the listener resists evaluative statements or solutions, active listening and observation skills can be used effectively to deal with such interactions.

Sample Answers

1. a. You are uncertain and puzzled about what is expected.
   b. You probably feel frustrated or discouraged about revising this report.
2. a. You are concerned about finishing the report by the deadline.
   b. You are feeling bogged down by all the work.
3. a. You are frustrated when I offer suggestions because of your experience with this job.
   b. You think that I distrust you when I give ideas on how to do your job.
4. a. You feel irritated that our meetings always start late.
   b. You are anxious to start our meetings on time.
5. a. You feel that Bill will not do his share if he is assigned to this project.
   b. You feel disappointed that I did not consult with you before the assignment.
   c. You feel afraid that your performance might be jeopardized as a member of this team.
6. a. You think that I am not responsible when I do not turn in my progress reports.
   b. You are irritated when my progress reports are late.
7. a. You are concerned that this new procedure will not work.
   b. You feel impatient when procedures that failed once are implemented again.
8. a. You are angry that our talking is disturbing others.
   b. You are afraid that our talking will keep others from doing their work.
9. a. You feel frustrated when your work load appears to change constantly.
   b. You feel discouraged because there is too much to do.
10. a. You are angry because you think that young people today are not as dedicated as you are.
    b. You feel discouraged about the lack of interest in this project.

253. PENNY PITCH: DEMONSTRATING REINFORCEMENT STYLES

Goals

 I. To demonstrate how positive or negative reinforcement can affect motivation and task accomplishment.

 II. To increase awareness of responses to interventions made by persons with position and status.

Group Size

Three teams of three to seven members each.

Time Required

Approximately one hour.

Materials

 I. Three different Penny Pitch Monitor Sheets, one for the monitor of each team.

 II. A pencil for each monitor.

 III. A stack of forty pennies for each group.

 IV. A small table for each group, located near the pitching area.

 V. Wide masking tape.

Physical Setting

A large room in which the three teams can carry out their tasks without overhearing the comments made by the monitors or the facilitator to the other teams. There must be three walls available that are suitable for the Penny Pitch activity (see Directions for Marking a Penny Pitch Area). Three separate rooms, one for each team, is preferable.

Process

 I. All participants are assembled in one room. The facilitator introduces the activity:

"You may have heard of the childhood game of 'pitching pennies.' The intent is to toss a penny against a wall and have it ricochet and land as close as possible to a line that runs parallel to the wall. In our case, the line is indicated by masking tape. The tape is six inches from the wall and is two feet long."

II. He informs the participants of the rules for the activity:
   1. Each participant will be asked to report only the score for his best toss.
   2. A participant may stop tossing at any time after he scores a "hit" on the tape, or may keep tossing, regardless of his scores, up to *forty* tosses.

III. The facilitator selects three members to serve as monitors. He takes them aside and gives each of them one of the three different Penny Pitch Monitor Sheets and a pencil. He briefly outlines the goals of the activity for them and allows them a few moments to study their instructions.

IV. While the monitors are reading their instructions, the facilitator divides the participants into three teams. He indicates to each team where its Penny Pitch area is (the areas have been marked off previously by the facilitator, according to the Directions for Marking a Penny Pitch Area). The facilitator also shows to each team the stack of forty pennies on the table near its pitching area.

V. A monitor is assigned to each team, and the Penny Pitch begins. Each member of a team pitches in turn, with all three teams engaged simultaneously. The monitor for each team records the best scores of the members; unknown to them, he also records how many pitches each one attempts *after* he scores a correct "hit" by causing a penny to *ricochet* onto the tape. The monitors also carry out the instructions on their Penny Pitch Monitor Sheets regarding their reactions to team members' performances.

VI. While the teams are pitching, the facilitator casually moves from team to team, using the same kind of reinforcement with each group as the monitor does, i.e., positive with the first group, no comments but merely observation with the second group, and negative with the last group.

VII. When all team members have finished pitching pennies, the total group is reassembled. The facilitator then states the goals of the activity. He says that the people who have received positive reinforcement will usually keep tossing even after they have scored a "hit"; the people who were criticized usually will quit after they have hit the tape and refuse to toss any more. The persons who were virtually ignored by the observers will usually fall somewhere in between.

VIII. The monitors report on the frequency or pattern of pitching for their teams. The impact of the facilitator's joining in the reinforcement is discussed.

Group members are encouraged to report how they felt during the experience and why they responded as they did. The facilitator then leads a general discussion of how behavior is affected by social reinforcement in real-life situations, and group members are encouraged to give examples from their own back-home situations.

Variations

I. More powerful data is generated if participants are brought into the room one at a time to pitch pennies. The facilitator then gives positive reinforcement to the first participant, negative reinforcement to the second, and no reinforcement to the third, and so on, while he notes the participant's reactions and the amount of time that persons receiving each type of reinforcement spend in the room. Participants are told not to discuss the experience with others until the general discussion. This variation allows the facilitator complete control over the reinforcement given.

II. A second round can be held, in the form of a competition between members of all three teams. Members take turns shooting in one area. Each individual may take up to ten shots; only the best toss counts; low score wins. Pennies are available in one or two other Penny Pitch areas, and team members are told that they may practice. While the facilitator oversees the competition, the monitors note intergroup competition and the types of reinforcing or criticizing behaviors adopted by the participants. Do they direct anger at the monitors and facilitator? How do the teams deal with success or failure? Are these reactions related to the type of reinforcement they received in the first part of the experience?

Similar Structured Experiences: *'73 Annual:* Structured Experiences **98, 100;** *Vol. V:* **154, 159, 162;** *Vol. VI:* **204, 207, 210.**

Suggested Instruments: *Vol. I:* "T-P Leadership Questionnaire"; *'72 Annual:* "Supervisory Attitudes: The X-Y Scale"; *'73 Annual:* "Motivation Feedback Opinionnaire," "LEAD (Leadership: Employee Orientation and Differentiation Questionnaire)"; *'75 Annual:* "Diagnosing Organization Ideology"; *'76 Annual:* "Leader Effectiveness and Adaptability Description (LEAD)"; *'78 Annual:* "Mach V Attitude Inventory."

Lecturette Sources: *'72 Annual:* "McGregor's Theory X-Theory Y Model"; *'76 Annual:* "Leadership as Persuasion and Adaptation," "Power"; *'77 Annual:* "Intervening in Organizations Through Reward Systems"; *'79 Annual:* "A Practical Model of Motivation and Character Development."

Submitted by Bradford F. Spencer.

Notes on the Use of "Penny Pitch":

DIRECTIONS FOR MARKING A PENNY PITCH AREA

Against three straight walls in the room, set up three Penny Pitch areas, one for each group. In each area, attach a strip of wide masking tape to the floor—the tape is two feet long and runs parallel to the wall, six inches from it. Each area should contain a small table to hold the group's supply of pennies for pitching.

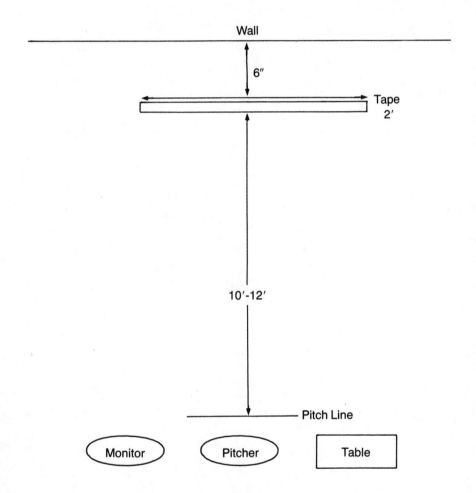

If three rooms are available, a pitching area can be set up in each room. This will ensure that the teams do not overhear each other.

PENNY PITCH MONITOR SHEET #1

The goal of this activity is to show how positive or negative reinforcement can affect task accomplishment and motivation.

You will be assigned to monitor one of three teams as the members pitch pennies. (The rules for pitching will be explained by the facilitator.) The members of your team are to believe only that you will be recording each participant's scores. However, in addition to that function, you will perform *two* additional tasks without the group members' knowledge:

1. You are to record *how many times* each team member pitches after he scores a "hit" on the tape.
2. While each member of your team is pitching pennies, you are to encourage the pitcher by reinforcing task-related performance, e.g., "Great toss, you are doing very well," "You are really improving," "I am glad you are on my team," "Hey, you could go professional," etc.

PENNY PITCH MONITOR SHEET #2

The goal of this activity is to show how positive or negative reinforcement can affect task accomplishment and motivation.

You will be assigned to monitor one of three teams as the members pitch pennies. (The rules for pitching will be explained by the facilitator.) The members of your team are to believe only that you will be recording each participant's scores. However, in addition to that function, you will perform *two* additional tasks without the group members' knowledge:

1. You are to record *how many times* each team member pitches after he scores a "hit" on the tape.
2. While each member of your team is pitching pennies, you are not to comment on the member's performance. If you are required to say something, try to make it as neutral a remark as possible (neither positive nor negative).

PENNY PITCH MONITOR SHEET   #3

The goal of this activity is to show how positive or negative reinforcement can affect task accomplishment and motivation.

You will be assigned to monitor one of three teams as the members pitch pennies. (The rules for pitching will be explained by the facilitator.) The members of your team are to believe only that you will be recording each participant's scores. However, in addition to that function, you will perform *two* additional tasks without the group members' knowledge:

1. You are to record *how many times* each member pitches after he scores a "hit" on the tape.
2. While each member of your team is pitching pennies, you are to make negative comments about his performance, e.g., "Oh, that was an awful shot," "Ouch," "Most people do better than you by this point," "It's a good thing you don't have to make a living doing this!," etc.

254. STONES, BANDS, AND CIRCLE: SOCIOGRAM ACTIVITIES

Goals

I. To explore existing levels of interaction, influence, and inclusion in a group.

II. To develop an awareness of group dynamics.

Group Size

A maximum of thirty participants in an ongoing group.

Time Required

Approximately forty-five minutes to one hour per activity.

Materials

I. (For Pile of Stones) A collection of small stones—equal to approximately twice the number of participants—of varying color, size, shape, and texture.

II. Masking tape (optional).

III. Newsprint and a felt-tipped marker (optional for discussion).

Physical Setting

A room large enough to accommodate all group members moving about with space between them.

Process

Pile of Stones

I. The facilitator explains that members will create a symbolic "picture" of the group. He places a collection of stones in the middle of the group and directs that each participant is to examine the stones and then to select one stone that represents himself in the group. (Three to five minutes.)

II. Participants are told to study their own stones and to try to identify with them. While they are doing this, the facilitator clears away the unselected stones. (Three to five minutes.)

III. The facilitator says that each member's stone represents that person. He instructs the members to nonverbally create a diagram or "picture" of the group with the stones. Each person is to place his stone in terms of where the participant sees himself in the picture of the group: next to whom, in between or surrounded by whom, the distance between one's own stone and others, and inclusion in or distance from the majority of members in the group. The facilitator allows ten minutes for this activity and gives a two-minute warning signal before the time is up.

IV. The facilitator tells the participants to study the pattern of stones and then announces that each participant may now move his stone, without discussion, to more accurately reflect his position in the group. (Five minutes.)

V. The facilitator leads the participants in a discussion of how their stones represent them, how they feel about their positions in the design, whether these accurately reflect their "places" in the group, how their positions in the group reflect their influence over others or others' influence over them, and how their positions reflect who they interact with or feel close to in the group. (Fifteen minutes.)

VI. The facilitator now announces that any member may move his stone for the last time or ask another member to move that member's stone to a particular location. The person being asked may either comply with or refuse the request. (Five minutes.)

VII. The facilitator leads a discussion of the experience, focusing on finding one's place in the group, members' feelings about their positions and their relation to other members, and reactions to having members move away from them or being asked to assume a different place in the group. These symbolic expressions are then related to actual group dynamics.

Bands

I. The facilitator tells the group that the following activity will be nonverbal. He places a marker (any object) in the center of the room and designates it as the center or nucleus of the group, symbolizing the goals and purposes of the group.

II. The facilitator instructs the group members to imagine that there are rings or bands around the nucleus, larger and larger circles, about two feet apart. He directs the members to position themselves on these bands, either nearer or farther from the center of the group, depending on how closely their own goals and interests match the goals and interests of the group. He reminds them that the experience is nonverbal.

III. When members have positioned themselves, the facilitator instructs them to remain on the bands on which they are standing (i.e., distance from the center) but to attempt to move closer to people for whom they feel the greatest interpersonal attraction and farther away from those for whom they feel the most interpersonal distance by moving around the band. Members can also face toward or away from other members to indicate positive and negative attractions. The facilitator tells them that they will have five minutes to reposition themselves and that there is to be no talking during this phase.

IV. The facilitator tells the participants that without changing their positions on the bands or the directions they are facing, they are to indicate how much impact or control they have in the group by standing (most impact), kneeling (medium impact), or sitting (least impact) in position.

V. The facilitator tells the participants to remain in the places they are and begins a group discussion of the experience. Members are encouraged to describe their feelings about their positions and the positions of others in relation to them in terms of inclusion, influence, and distance.

VI. After approximately ten minutes of discussion, the facilitator announces that members are released from their bands and positions if they choose to be. Any member may move within the group space, but will be requested to explain such a move to the member he moves away from and the member he moves toward, including any changes in feeling that result from the move. The facilitator continues to lead the group in a discussion of members' positions in relation to actual group dynamics. He may focus on how the places or positions assumed by members impact and reflect individual and group interests and goals.

Circle

I. The facilitator indicates an imaginary circle (large enough to accommodate all group members) within the room and says that the edges of the circle are the limits of the group's existence—all group interactions take place within the circle.

II. He directs the participants to stand within the circle and tells them to concentrate on here-and-now behaviors, feelings, and needs while they mill about within the circle.

III. After one minute, the facilitator directs each participant to place himself physically in a position that best describes his relationship to the group and individual members. (Five minutes.)

IV. The facilitator describes (without interpreting) the position of each participant in turn; he solicits from that participant one word that best describes his or her own feelings at the moment. (Ten to fifteen minutes.)

V. The facilitator leads a group discussion of the existing interpersonal relationships and interactions between group members. (Five to ten minutes.)

VI. The facilitator instructs the members to mill about within the circle for a minute and then to place themselves in what they would consider to be an *ideal* position within the group.

VII. Group members are directed to discuss with the rest of the members their new positions and the feelings that are associated with these positions. The facilitator observes this interaction. (Ten to fifteen minutes.)

VIII. The facilitator assembles the group and leads a diagnosis of the interpersonal dynamics, group interpersonal weaknesses, group interpersonal strengths, and adequacy of the group structure to carry out tasks. He mentions the implications of the impact of the inclusion, influence, and closeness that he has witnessed on individual and group goals. He then leads a group discussion of interpersonal needs and the expectations of the group in terms of group structure and group dynamics.

Similar Structured Experiences: *Vol. I:* Structured Experiences **22, 23;** *Vol. II:* **37, 38, 39;** *Vol. III:* **55, 57, 58, 72;** *'72 Annual:* **86;** *Vol. IV:* **113;** *'77 Annual:* **196;** *Vol. VI:* **208.**

Suggested Instruments: *Vol. III:* "Group-Climate Inventory," "Group-Growth Evaluation Form," "Group-Behavior Questionnaire"; *'72 Annual:* "TORI Group Self-Diagnosis Scale"; *'77 Annual:* "Current Status Inventory."

Lecturette Sources: *'72 Annual:* "TORI Theory and Practice"; *'73 Annual:* "A Model of Group Development"; *'74 Annual:* "Hidden Agendas," "Cogs Ladder: A Model of Group Development"; *'76 Annual:* "Yin/Yang: A Perspective on Theories of Group Development"; *'77 Annual:* "D-I-D: A Three-Dimensional Model for Understanding Group Communication," "A Tavistock Primer."

Notes on the Use of "Stones, Bands, and Circle":

"Pile of Stones" submitted by Donald E. Miskiman. "Bands" submitted by John E. Hoover and Melvin A. Goldstein. "Circle" submitted by Donald Anderson.

255. LISTS: A COLLECTION OF CONSENSUS ACTIVITIES

Goals

    I. To allow participants to practice giving and receiving feedback.

    II. To practice effective consensus-seeking behavior in groups.

    III. To demonstrate that relevant performance data from interdependent tasks is widely rather than narrowly shared by group members.

Group Size

    Three to five groups of five or six members each.

Time Required

    Two and one-half to three hours.

Materials

    I. A copy of one of the following work sheets for each participant:
        1. Lists Business Performance Individual Work Sheet
        2. Lists Human Fears Individual Work Sheet
        3. Lists Most Populous Countries Individual Work Sheet. (Other lists that can be rank ordered can be used.)

    II. A copy of one of the following work sheets for each group:
        1. Lists Business Performance Group Work Sheet
        2. Lists Human Fears Group Work Sheet
        3. Lists Most Populous Countries Group Work Sheet.

    III. A copy of the Lists Score Sheet for each participant.

    IV. A pencil for each participant.

    V. Newsprint and a felt-tipped marker.

Physical Setting

    A room that is large enough for each group to work separately without being overheard by the other groups, or a separate room for each group, and a writing surface for each participant.

Process

I. The facilitator introduces the activity as one that will look at individual and group decision making and feedback.

II. The facilitator gives each participant a copy of the same one of the three individual work sheets and a pencil and tells them to individually rank order the items according to the directions provided. (Ten minutes.)

III. Groups of five to six persons each are formed. The facilitator distributes to each group a copy of the group work sheet that corresponds to the individual work sheet just completed. The groups are given the task of deriving a ranking by group consensus for the group work sheet. The facilitator stresses that there must be substantial agreement among group members on the rank assigned to each item: no averaging or "majority-rule" voting is allowed.

IV. The facilitator directs each group to select a manager. He says that the manager may exercise whatever authority he deems necessary and will participate in the group process. The facilitator directs the groups to begin the ranking task. (Thirty minutes.)

V. The facilitator calls time. He distributes a Lists Score Sheet to each member and directs participants in scoring according to the directions given on the sheet. When this task is completed, the *average individual scores* for each item and the group scores for each item are posted on newsprint.

V. The total group is reassembled, and the facilitator leads a discussion of the average of individual scores compared with the range of group scores.[1] They then discuss group resources compared with individual resources and the extent to which these resources were used in the groups.

VII. Participants break into their small groups again, and each group manager critiques his group's performance. He also critiques or evaluates each individual member's performance.

VIII. Each member of the group is then told that he has the same task as the manager: to critique the performance of the group, including the manager and the effect that the manager had on the group-consensus process. Group members take turns doing this. (One-half hour.)

---

[1]For a discussion of the scoring procedure, see Dennis P. Slevin, "Observations on the Invalid Scoring Algorithm of 'NASA' and Similar Consensus Tasks." *Group & Organization Studies*, 3(4), 497-507.

IX. The large group readjourns, and the facilitator leads a discussion of the experience. Members are encouraged to share their feelings and reactions to giving and receiving feedback, what they learned about themselves in the feedback process, what they learned about the group-consensus process, and what learnings they can apply to other group experiences.

Variations

I. Money can be used as a reward for performance. In this case, each manager would disburse the "reward" money to group members as part of his evaluation of their performance. Each member could then disagree with the manager's evaluation, but his decisions about money disbursement would stand.

II. Step VIII can be omitted.

III. There can be no group manager; instead, members critique each other's performances.

IV. Other rank-ordered lists can be used (see Similar Structured Experiences).

Similar Structured Experiences: *Vol. I:* Structured Experience 11; *Vol. II:* **30;** *Vol. III:* **55, 60, 64, 69;** *Vol. IV:* **115;** *'75 Annual:* **140, 146;** *Vol. V:* **157;** *'76 Annual:* **177;** *'78 Annual:* **222, 223.**

Suggested Instruments: *Vol. III:* "Group-Climate Inventory," "Group-Growth Evaluation Form," "Group-Behavior Questionnaire"; *'75 Annual:* "Decision-Style Inventory."

Lecturette Sources: *'72 Annual:* "Openness, Collusion and Feedback"; *'73 Annual:* "Synergy and Consensus Seeking"; *'75 Annual:* "Applied Group Problem Solving: The Nominal Group Technique," "Giving Feedback: An Interpersonal Skill"; *'76 Annual:* "Interpersonal Feedback as Consensual Validation of Constructs," "Making Judgments Descriptive"; *'78 Annual:* "Utilizing Human Resources: Individual Versus Group Approaches to Problem Solving and Decision Making."

Notes on the Use of "Lists":

Based on material submitted by Barry D. Leskin.

ANSWER KEYS

I. Busines Performance (average ratings on a scale from 7 [excellent] to 1 [poor])[2]

1. Airlines (5.47)
2. Aluminum companies (5.02)
3. Banks (4.93)
4. Savings and loan associations (4.91)
5. Large department stores (4.77)
6. Retail food chains (4.72)
7. Forestry companies (4.71)
8. Wine producers (4.57)
9. Appliance manufacturers (4.56)
10. Tire manufacturers (4.55)
11. Telephone companies (4.50)
11. Food manufacturers (4.50)
13. Plastics companies (4.40)
14. Prescription-drug manufacturers (4.35)
15. Liquor distillers (4.33)
16. Electric utilities (4.31)
16. Life-insurance companies (4.31)
16. Steel manufacturers (4.31)
19. Building-materials companies (4.20)
20. Chemical companies (4.14)
21. Gas utilities (4.08)
22. Gasoline service stations (3.94)
23. Property/casualty-insurance companies (3.87)
24. Nonprescription-drug manufacturers (3.83)
25. Oil and gasoline companies (3.72)
26. Automobile manufacturers (3.66)
27. Medical/hospitalization-insurance companies (3.53)
28. Railroads (3.51)
29. Automobile dealers (3.44)
30. Appliance-repair services (3.42)
31. Automobile-insurance companies (3.35)

II. Human Fears[3]

1. Speaking before a group
2. Heights
3. Insects and bugs
3. Financial problems
3. Deep water
6. Sickness
6. Death
8. Flying
9. Loneliness
10. Dogs
11. Driving/riding in a car
12. Darkness
12. Elevators
14. Escalators

---

[2]Reprinted from *U.S. News & World Report*, February 20, 1978, p. 17. Copyright 1978 U.S. News & World Report, Inc.

[3]Reprinted from *The Sunday Times*. London: October 7, 1973.

III. Most Populous Countries (Census Bureau estimates—multiply by 1,000)[4]

1. People's Republic of China (982,531)
2. India (643,040)
3. Union of Soviet Socialist Republics (258,900)
4. United States (216,817)
5. Indonesia (141,670)
6. Brazil (118,789)
7. Japan (113,860)
8. Bangladesh (83,511)
9. Pakistan (75,472)
10. Nigeria (66,628)
11. Mexico (63,686)
12. Federal Republic of (West) Germany (61,392)
13. Italy (56,436)
14. United Kingdom (55,956)
15. France (53,103)
16. Viet Nam (49,948)
17. Philippines (44,863)
18. Thailand (44,694)
19. Turkey (41,759)
20. Egypt (38,831)
21. Republic of (South) Korea (38,195)
22. Iran (37,121)
23. Spain (36,351)
24. Poland (34,698)
25. Burma (31,958)

---

[4]Source: U.S. Bureau of the Census, Population Division, "World Population, 1977," in press.

LISTS BUSINESS PERFORMANCE INDIVIDUAL WORK SHEET

Introduction: The second annual "Study of American Opinion," sponsored at the end of 1977 by *U.S. News & World Report* and conducted by Marketing Concepts, Inc., reveals the public's assessment of American business. Although the 5,873 American respondents believed in free, private enterprise, they named business'es lack of interest in communicating honestly with or providing value to the consumer as primary sources of their dissatisfaction.

Instructions: Below is a list of thirty-one major industries. Your task is to rank them in the order in which the survey respondents ranked their performance, from "1" (best) to "31" (worst).

_____ Airlines
_____ Aluminum companies
_____ Appliance manufacturers
_____ Appliance-repair services
_____ Automobile dealers
_____ Automobile-insurance companies
_____ Automobile manufacturers
_____ Banks
_____ Building-materials companies
_____ Chemical companies
_____ Electric utilities
_____ Food manufacturers
_____ Forestry companies
_____ Gas utilities
_____ Gasoline service stations
_____ Large department stores
_____ Life-insurance companies

_____ Liquor distillers
_____ Medical/hospitalization-insurance companies
_____ Nonprescription-drug manufacturers
_____ Oil and gasoline companies
_____ Plastics companies
_____ Prescription-drug manufacturers
_____ Property/casualty-insurance companies
_____ Railroads
_____ Retail food chains
_____ Savings and loan associations
_____ Steel manufacturers
_____ Telephone companies
_____ Tire manufacturers
_____ Wine producers

LISTS BUSINESS PERFORMANCE GROUP WORK SHEET

Instructions: Your group is to employ the group-consensus method in reaching its decisions. This means that rankings must be agreed on, at least partially, by each group member. Here are some guidelines to use in reaching consensus:

1. Approach the task on the basis of logic. Avoid arguing for your own individual judgments.
2. Avoid changing your mind only to reach agreement and avoid conflict. Support only solutions with which you can agree at least somewhat.
3. Avoid techniques such as majority voting, averaging, or trading in order to reduce conflict and reach a decision.
4. View differences of opinion as an asset, rather than a hindrance, in group decision making.

Rank the industries listed below in the order in which you think survey respondents ranked their performance, from "1" (best) to "31" (worst).

_____Airlines
_____Aluminum companies
_____Appliance manufacturers
_____Appliance-repair services
_____Automobile dealers
_____Automobile-insurance
companies
_____Automobile manufacturers
_____Banks
_____Building-materials companies
_____Chemical companies
_____Electric utilities
_____Food manufacturers
_____Forestry companies
_____Gas utilities
_____Gasoline service stations
_____Large department stores
_____Life-insurance companies

_____Liquor distillers
_____Medical/hospitalization-
insurance companies
_____Nonprescription-drug
manufacturers
_____Oil and gasoline companies
_____Plastics companies
_____Prescription-drug manufacturers
_____Property/casualty-insurance
companies
_____Railroads
_____Retail food chains
_____Savings and loan associations
_____Steel manufacturers
_____Telephone companies
_____Tire manufacturers
_____Wine producers

LISTS HUMAN FEARS INDIVIDUAL WORK SHEET

Introduction: The Sunday Times (London, October 7, 1973) reported a survey conducted by market researchers among 3,000 inhabitants of the United States. The question asked was "What are you the most afraid of?"

Instructions: Below is a list of fourteen common fears. Your task is to rank them in the order in which the survey respondents mentioned them most, from "1" (most feared) to "14" (least feared).

_____ Darkness   _____ Financial problems
_____ Death   _____ Flying
_____ Deep water   _____ Heights
_____ Dogs   _____ Insects and bugs
_____ Driving/riding in a car   _____ Loneliness
_____ Elevators   _____ Sickness
_____ Escalators   _____ Speaking before a group

LISTS HUMAN FEARS GROUP WORK SHEET

Instructions: Your group is to employ the group-consensus method in reaching its decisions. This means that rankings must be agreed on, at least partially, by each group member. Here are some guidelines to use in reaching consensus:

1. Approach the task on the basis of logic. Avoid arguing for your own individual judgments.
2. Avoid changing your mind only to reach agreement and avoid conflict. Support only solutions with which you can agree at least somewhat.
3. Avoid techniques such as majority voting, averaging, or trading in order to reduce conflict and reach a decision.
4. View differences of opinion as an asset, rather than a hindrance, in group decision making.

Rank the fears listed below in the order in which you think survey respondents mentioned them most, from "1" (most feared) to "14" (least feared).

_____ Darkness   _____ Financial problems
_____ Death   _____ Flying
_____ Deep water   _____ Heights
_____ Dogs   _____ Insects and bugs
_____ Driving/riding in a car   _____ Loneliness
_____ Elevators   _____ Sickness
_____ Escalators   _____ Speaking before a group

LISTS MOST POPULOUS COUNTRIES INDIVIDUAL WORK SHEET

Introduction: The U.S. Bureau of the Census has identified the twenty-five countries in the world that contained the most people as of July, 1977.

Instructions: Below is a list of the twenty-five most populous countries. Your task is to rank them in the order of greatest population (1) through lowest population (25).

_____ Bangladesh
_____ Brazil
_____ Burma
_____ Egypt
_____ Federal Republic of (West) Germany
_____ France
_____ India
_____ Indonesia
_____ Iran
_____ Italy
_____ Japan
_____ Mexico
_____ Nigeria

_____ Pakistan
_____ People's Republic of China
_____ Philippines
_____ Poland
_____ Republic of (South) Korea
_____ Spain
_____ Thailand
_____ Turkey
_____ Union of Soviet Socialist Republics
_____ United Kingdom
_____ United States
_____ Viet Nam

LISTS MOST POPULOUS COUNTRIES GROUP WORK SHEET

Instructions: Your group is to employ the group-consensus method in reaching its decisions. This means that rankings must be agreed on, at least partially, by each group member. Here are some guidelines to use in reaching consensus:

1. Approach the task on the basis of logic. Avoid arguing for your own individual judgments.
2. Avoid changing your mind only to reach agreement and avoid conflict. Support only solutions with which you can agree at least somewhat.
3. Avoid techniques such as majority voting, averaging, or trading in order to reduce conflict and reach a decision.
4. View differences of opinion as an asset, rather than a hindrance, in group decision making.

Rank the countries listed below in order of greatest population (1) through lowest population (25).

_____ Bangladesh
_____ Brazil
_____ Burma
_____ Egypt
_____ Federal Republic of (West) Germany
_____ France
_____ India
_____ Indonesia
_____ Iran
_____ Italy
_____ Japan
_____ Mexico
_____ Nigeria

_____ Pakistan
_____ People's Republic of China
_____ Philippines
_____ Poland
_____ Republic of (South) Korea
_____ Spain
_____ Thailand
_____ Turkey
_____ Union of Soviet Socialist Republics
_____ United Kingdom
_____ United States
_____ Viet Nam

LISTS SCORE SHEET

This scoring form can be used with any consensus-seeking task that involves rank ordering a list of items that has a "correct" ranking according to some external criterion. It may appear formidable, but it is really simple arithmetic.

Instructions: In column (a) copy the ranks you assigned to the individual items. Then your group calculates the average of the individuals' ranks for each item and records this (one decimal place) in column (b). In (c), copy the ranks assigned by your group through consensus. The facilitator will call out the "correct" rankings, which you will copy into column (d). Take the difference between columns (a) and (d), make it a positive numeral (+) and record it in column (e) for each item. The differences between columns (b) and (d) are recorded (all +) in column (f), and the differences between columns (c) and (d) (all +) are noted in column (g). Add up columns (e), (f), and (g) to obtain your error score, your group's average error score, and the error score for group consensus.

Item	(a) Your Ranking	(b) Average of Individual Ranks	(c) Your Group's Ranking	(d) Correct Ranking	(e) a-d (all +)	(f) b-d (all +)	(g) c-d (all +)
1							
2							
3							
4							
5							
6							
7							
8							
9							
10							
11							
12							
13							
14							
15							
16							
17							
18							

Item	(a) Your Ranking	(b) Average of Individual Ranks	(c) Your Group's Ranking	(d) Correct Ranking	(e) a-d (all +)	(f) b-d (all +)	(g) c-d (all +)
19							
20							
21							
22							
23							
24							
25							
26							
27							
28							
29							
30							
31							

Total   _____   _____   _____

     Your   *Group*   *Consensus*
     Error   *Average*   *Error*
     Score   *Error*   *Score*
                 Score

Best Individual Score _____

256. SLINGSHOTS: STUDYING GROUP DYNAMICS

Goals

I. To experience the group dynamics involved in task accomplishment.

II. To study the effects of competition on group functioning.

III. To experience the functional and dysfunctional aspects of process interventions.

Group Size

Any number of groups of eight to ten members each.

Time Required

Approximately one hour and fifteen minutes.

Materials

I. A copy of the Slingshots Workers' Instruction Sheet for each member.

II. A piece of blank paper and a pencil for each consultant.

III. One set of Master Builder Tinkertoys for each group.

IV. Two pairs of small, inefficient children's scissors for each group.

V. One box of No. 105 rubber bands (approximately five-inch bands) for each group.

VI. Three pieces of fabric (approximately 12″ x 12″ each) for cutting slingshot pockets (old handkerchiefs work well) for each group.

VII. Newsprint and a felt-tipped marker.

Physical Setting

A long table with six chairs along one side of it must be provided for *each* group in the "assembly" room, which must be large enough to accommodate all groups. A separate room, to which all workers can be sent, also is required.

Process

I. The facilitator forms the groups. He places the materials for each group on the tables, as he tells the members that six of them in each group will produce slingshots made out of Tinkertoys while the remaining group members will act as consultants. He directs each group to select six workers and tells the workers to seat themselves along one side of their group's assembly table. In seating order, they are designated as workers 1, 2, 3, 4, 5, and 6.

II. The facilitator distributes copies of the Slingshots Workers' Instruction Sheet to all members. He tells the workers that they will have ten minutes to read their instructions and then ten minutes to assemble as many slingshots as possible. The consultants are instructed to observe the assembly process but to say nothing. At the end of the allotted time, the number of slingshots completed by each group is recorded by the facilitator on newsprint, then the Tinkertoy pieces are disassembled by the consultants to provide raw materials for the next round. Rubber bands and cloth pockets are cut and assembled anew by the workers during each round.

III. The facilitator directs the workers into another room. He tells the consultants that they have ten minutes as a group in which to redesign the assembly line for their group, switch tasks, double up on tasks, etc., as they see fit.

IV. The workers are called back into the assembly room, and the new production operation is explained to each group of workers by the consultants for that group. (Five minutes.)

V. The workers are given ten minutes to assemble as many slingshots as possible under their new guidelines. At the end of the production period, the completed units are again counted and recorded, then disassembled, and new rubber bands and fabric are provided.

VI. The facilitator announces that the workers themselves have ten minutes in which to redesign their jobs. The consultants can serve as observers during this process but are not to participate or comment.

VII. A third ten-minute production period is conducted, with workers operating under the production procedures that they have established. The number of completed slingshots is recorded.

VIII. The facilitator leads the entire group in a discussion of the experience. Dynamics of each round are discussed in terms of production outcome as well as the workers' feelings about each production effort. Any element of competition between the workers and the consultants is explored as well as what was helpful or hindering about the consultants' interventions. Finally, the applications of the learnings gained are applied to typical work situations.

Variations

I. Videotaping the production run allows group members to observe how group relationships changed during the activity.

II. Groups can compete with each other.

III. Members can be instructed to add a new dimension (decoration, etc.) to the slingshots during the last round.

Similar Structured Experiences: *Vol. I:* Structured Experience **10;** *Vol. II:* **32, 37;** *'72 Annual:* **79, 81;** *Vol. V:* **161, 163;** *'77 Annual:* **194;** *'78 Annual:* **228;** *'79 Annual:* **243.**

Suggested Instruments: *Vol. III:* "Group-Climate Inventory," "Group-Behavior Questionnaire."

Lecturette Sources: *'73 Annual:* "A Model of Group Development"; *'74 Annual:* "Models and Roles of Change Agents"; *'76 Annual:* "Role Functions in a Group"; *'78 Annual:* "Tolerance of Equivocality: The Bronco, Easy Rider, Blockbuster, and Nomad."

Notes on the Use of "Slingshots":

Submitted by Kenneth M. Bond.

SLINGSHOTS WORKERS' INSTRUCTION SHEET

Instructions: Your group's task is to produce as many completed slingshot units as possible in a ten-minute period. Each group member will be responsible for one production-line assembly task, as delineated below:

Worker 1: Trace and cut out rectangular slingshot pockets.
Worker 2: Loop two rubber bands together for each slingshot.
Worker 3: Attach rubber-band pair to cloth pocket to form slingshot propulsion system.
Worker 4: Attach blue peg to center of round spool to form base of unit.
Worker 5: Insert two yellow rods into second spool at 90° angle to form top of unit and attach blue rod of base into center of top spool.
Worker 6: Attach rubber bands of propulsion system to yellow rods at top of unit.

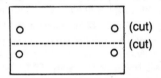

Fabric slingshot pocket

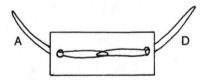

Lay one rubber band next to the other with end C overlapping on *top* of end B. Loop end D through the top of the space between B and C and pull taut.

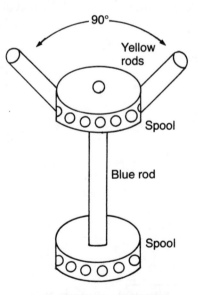

A\   D

Push ends A and B through holes in (back of) fabric pocket. Ends A and B are looped and twisted, each over one of the yellow rods on the slingshot base assembly.

Rubber band/pocket assembly

Slingshot base assembly

257. SUNGLOW: AN APPRAISAL ROLE PLAY

Goals

  I. To practice skills in counseling, coaching, and active listening.

  II. To increase awareness of behavioral and interpersonal factors that influence an interview.

  III. To provide feedback on interviewing effectiveness.

Group Size

Two groups of four to six members each. (Additional participants serve as process observers.)

Time Required

Two to two and one-half hours.

Materials

  I. A copy of the Sunglow Background Information Sheet for each participant.

  II. A copy of the Sunglow Employee Background Data Sheet and a copy of the Sunglow Appraisal Report Sheet for each member of the managerial team.

  III. A copy of the Sunglow Employee Biography Sheet for each member of the employee team.

  IV. A copy of the Sunglow Interview-Skills Observer Sheet for each observer.

  V. A pencil for each participant.

  VI. Newsprint and a felt-tipped marker.

Physical Setting

A room large enough to contain all participants in two face-to-face teams and two separate rooms in which the teams can read and discuss their roles.

Process

  I. The facilitator gives a lecturette on the skills required in appraisal interviewing. He may elicit such a list from the participants and post it.

II. The participants are divided into two groups of equal size, each containing four or six members. Additional participants act as observers. One group collectively is designated as the employee, Fredrich van den Nerk; the other group collectively represents the engineering manager, J. C. Rist.

III. Each participant is given a copy of the Sunglow Background Information Sheet and a pencil. Each member of the managerial team receives a copy of the Sunglow Employee Background Data Sheet and a copy of the Sunglow Appraisal Report Sheet. Each member of the employee team receives a copy of the Sunglow Employee Biography Sheet. Each observer receives a copy of the Sunglow Interview-Skills Observer Sheet.

IV. The facilitator explains that all senior staff employees in the Sunglow Petroleum Co. Ltd. are formally appraised once each year by their immediate supervisors. The ultimate purpose of the appraisals, according to the company's guide for managers, is "to ensure that each member of the staff makes the optimum contribution to profit improvement within his or her power and to help the individual attain the highest possible satisfaction from the job. The two aims are interrelated." (The facilitator may wish to write this goal on newsprint and post it where all participants can see it.) The facilitator adds that the completed appraisal reports are ultimately sent to the company's central office, where they serve as the basis for decisions on staff transfers and promotions. The object of the appraisal interview is "to assess the employee's performance over the past year as comprehensively and constructively as possible, to discuss and analyze with the employee those factors that have influenced his performance, and to establish a plan of action for the year to come."

V. The facilitator directs the managerial team and the employee team to their separate rooms and tells them that they have one-half hour in which to read the data and discuss the situation. He tells them that they will *not* elect a representative for the interview but that all will play the part of manager or employee, as though each member represented a part of that individual's personality. In this way several different ways of approaching the interview, for both the manager and the employee, may be tried and processed in the shortest possible time.

VI. After one-half hour, the managerial team is instructed to call the employee team into the large room, and the interview begins.

VII. After thirty to forty-five minutes the facilitator stops the interview and leads the participants in a review of the experience. He encourages the managers and employees to give feedback to each other. Observers then give their reports. The facilitator solicits examples of helpful and hindering behaviors during the interview and of counseling, coaching, and listening skills used by participants. The group members are encouraged to generalize some learnings about interviewing and to suggest how these could be applied in real-life situations.

Variations

I. The role play can be followed by a short lecture on transactional analysis and the interview role played once more with each party trying to remain in the Adult ego state. This second role play can involve individual managers and employees, with observers noting the extent to which both parties communicate clearly, listen actively, and stay in their "Adult" in the TA sense of the term. The effect on the outcome of the interview of Adult-Adult exchanges versus Parent-Child exchanges can be emphasized.

II. Videotape can be used to replay the interview before step VII.

III. The role play can be done in triads (employee, supervisor, observer).

IV. The supervisor and employee can reverse roles half-way through the interview.

V. New information about the employee can be introduced into the process.

Similar Structured Experiences: *Vol. I:* Structured Experience **8;** *Vol. III:* **52;** *'74 Annual:* **131;** *'75 Annual:* **142;** *'77 Annual:* **191;** *Vol. VI:* **219;** *'79 Annual:* **238;** *Vol. VII:* **252.**

Suggested Instruments: *'72 Annual:* "Supervisory Attitudes: The X-Y Scale"; *'73 Annual:* "Helping Relationships Inventory"; *'78 Annual:* "Critical Consulting Incidents Inventory (CCII)."

Lecturette Sources: *'72 Annual:* "Job Enrichment," "Management by Objectives"; *'73 Annual:* "The Sensing Interview"; *'75 Annual:* "The Supervisor as Counselor," "Giving Feedback: An Interpersonal Skill"; *'77 Annual:* "Organizational Norms."

Notes on the Use of "Sunglow":

Submitted by J. Malcolm Rigby.

SUNGLOW BACKGROUND INFORMATION SHEET

Sunglow Petroleum Co. Ltd. is a multinational company engaged in the exploration, production, and refining of petroleum products.

One branch of Sunglow is an operating company situated in Dunia, a small
independent state in North Africa. Dunia consists mainly of jungle, with the
exception of a small coastal strip that runs the length of the country. There are
no facilities for higher education in Dunia, few other facilities, and it is surrounded on three sides by fairly hostile countries, jealous of the mineral wealth it
possesses.

For these reasons, the Sunglow management and specialists in Dunia are
practically all expatriate Europeans who live in an almost self-contained "camp"
in the middle of the oil field on the coastal strip. The "camp" contains some five
hundred company houses, a company hospital and medical service, and a company supermarket that sells European goods. There are also a company club,
around which the social and sporting activities of the expatriates center, and a
company school for children up to twelve years of age.

Sunglow employees live for twelve months in Dunia along with their families
and are then allowed two months leave in their country of origin. All traveling
expenses for the employee and his family from Dunia are paid for by the company,
and full salary is paid during leave.

The original oil discoveries in Dunia, along the coastal strip, are now almost
worked out, and all the large and complex projects currently underway in the
company are in the offshore waters, from the surf zone to as far as fifty miles out.
The Dunia operation is regarded by the central office as a training ground for
proving young talent and is also one of the most profitable of the parent company's
many exploration ventures.

SUNGLOW EMPLOYEE BACKGROUND DATA SHEET

Fredrich (Fred) van den Nerk is thirty-four years old. He is a graduate in mechanical engineering from the University of Delft in Holland, a university with the reputation of producing the best engineers in Europe. He has worked for the Sunglow company for nine years, first in Holland, later in Zaroma in the Far East, and, for the last twelve months, in Dunia.

Van den Nerk was extremely disappointed and angry when he first came to Dunia, since he found himself working as a planning engineer in the land facilities department—a job he had held in Zaroma for the past four years. Apparently someone in the central office (London) had told him that he would be working in offshore construction as a project engineer when he arrived in Dunia. Although your request had been for a land facilities engineer, you saw that the work was much less complex than that which Van den Nerk had carried out in Zaroma and, by making several staff moves, you managed to get him the job in offshore construction which he coveted.

Van den Nerk has been an extremely active member of the senior staff club and is currently the sports secretary and a member of the football team. Sometime last year he broke a leg during a game and was in a cast for a number of weeks.

His family, too, has suffered some bad luck. His only child, a five-year-old daughter, has been hospitalized following a boating accident, and only a few weeks ago both mother and daughter were flown back to Holland at Sunglow's expense so that the child could be examined by medical specialists.

Van den Nerk's work leaves much to be desired. During his time in offshore construction he has not reached his targets on several occasions when a little more effort, particularly in dealing with other departments, could, in your opinion, have achieved the desired results. Two specific cases involved the nondelivery of materials for the job and an unpleasant episode between the planning engineers and the barge engineer over a drawing alteration. Van den Nerk, in the middle, seemingly added to the problem rather than helped resolve it. In your opinion, a major part of a project engineer's job is to deal with such sources of friction and job holdups with a minimum of disruptive conflict, and to achieve project goals even though under the considerable pressure that is inevitably generated on these jobs.

All the additional information you need is contained in the draft of the appraisal report that you have written on Van den Nerk. Although you have completed this report, you can alter it following discussions with the subordinate. You currently see no reason why you should do so.

SUNGLOW APPRAISAL REPORT SHEET

A. Statistical Data

Name of Employee	Job Title	Period of Assessment
Van den Nerk, Fredrich	Design Engineer	February 1978 to February 1979

Division	Nationality	Qualifications
Engineering	Dutch	Grad. Mech. Eng., Delft, 1970

Date of Birth	Joined Company	Joined This Branch	Pension Date
10 January 1945	5 September 1970	10 February 1978	5 September 2005

Previous Jobs in Company	Branch	Date
Trainee Engineer	Holland Sunglow	Sept. 70—March 71
Assistant Design Engineer	Holland Sunglow	March 71—April 74
Planning Engineer—Land Facilities	Zaroma Sunglow	April 74—Feb. 78

B. Report on Performance

1. *Jobs Held Since Last Report:*
   Planning Engineer—Land Facilities
   Project Engineer—Offshore Engineering Construction

2. *Performance of Work:*
   Van den Nerk has been involved in a number of medium-sized projects such as planning and designing the new gaslift facilities for the Tenjambong Field and as project engineer for AGP-64B, in addition to numerous smaller projects such as improvements to the offshore compressors. He began his first year in the Dunia branch with enthusiasm and was transferred to project engineering

following his own request. However, this early promise has not been fulfilled on his new job.

When he has been able to concentrate on specific tasks of a "desk-bound" nature, Van den Nerk has often produced sound solutions, although he has tended to get caught up in detail and his work has an uneven quality. When required to resolve a number of problems concurrently, he has tended to shy away from the more difficult ones, thus not bringing his projects along in a systematic manner. He is also prone to neglect work that is not of high priority, and his output also leaves room for improvement.

Van den Nerk appears to have lost his early initiative, his reports are not up to standard for this type of job, and he seems neither to keep close watch over the projects for which he is responsible nor to be able to instill in others a willingness to cooperate.

---

3. *Targets/Task for Coming Year:*

Van den Nerk will be transferred back to planning engineering in the land facilities department where he will be given the opportunity to improve his performance on various small projects.

---

4. *Performance Rating:*

Excellent	☐
Very Good	☐
Competent Performance	☐
Minimum Acceptable	☒
Poor	☐

---

5. *Name of Evaluator:* J. C. Rist

Signature:

Date:

C. Report on Development

1. *Factors that May Promote or Limit Further Development:*

Technically Van den Nerk is a reasonably sound engineer, and—despite his dissatisfaction with his initial job here in Dunia—he performed well in land facilities during the first quarter of the year. However, he seems unable to concentrate for longer periods of time and does not possess the overview necessary for large-project responsibility. He seems to lack confidence in his own ability, as is manifested in his tendency to opt out of difficult situations, leaving them, through default, for others to identify and solve. Particularly, he does not seem able to translate his social skills into the work situation nor does he seem willing to spend time examining problems in the field. These failings have led to problems between himself, the barge supervisors, materials department, and members of engineering planning.

If he can increase his work output, he may become an adequate specialist design engineer, but his ability to handle larger projects or a management post must be suspect, based on this year's performance.

---

2. *Potential*—Expressed as Job Group from J.G. 6 (starting) to J.G. 1 (highest):

	Last Year	This Year
a. Current	J.G. 4	J.G. 4
b. Expected Within Three Years:	J.G. 3	J.G. 4
c. Ultimate Potential:	J.G. 1	J.G. 3

---

3. *Possible Jobs in the Short Term:*

Planning Engineer

---

4. *Possible Jobs in the Long Term:*

Specialist in design or planning. Broader management posts unlikely, based on current performance.

---

5. *Training Required:*

---

6. *Employee's Reactions:*

---

7. *Name of Evaluator:* J. C. Rist

Signature:

Date:

SUNGLOW EMPLOYEE BIOGRAPHY SHEET

You are Fredrich (Fred) van den Nerk, thirty-four years of age, a graduate mechanical engineer from Delft University in Holland. You are currently waiting to have your staff appraisal interview with Mr. Rist, your boss. As you wait you review the year and, from your point of view, you believe that you have overcome some fairly severe difficulties and have put in a solid year's work.

You came to Dunia with your wife and only child (a five-year-old girl) at the beginning of the year in the belief that you would be a project engineer in offshore construction, a job that you had requested at your last two staff appraisal interviews. On arriving in Dunia you were placed in the land facilities department as a planning engineer, a job you had held for four years in Zaroma before your transfer. You were extremely upset and angry about this "betrayal" and told this to your boss and to the personnel manager. You were told that a transfer to offshore construction would be arranged for you as soon as possible, assuming that you proved capable of the job.

Consequently, you accepted the post in the land facilities department and found that you could produce what was regarded as excellent work without much real effort. Settling into the camp, and with little work of a demanding nature to do, you joined the club football team and the squash league and took up water skiing and sailing. In your third month, you were elected sports secretary to the company club and began to build up and organize the sports sections, arranging various sporting tournaments with other teams and leagues both within and outside Dunia. As a consequence, the senior staff club and Dunia Sunglow have become well known in sporting circles throughout the region, and you believe this has been good publicity for the company—even inducing young Dunians who may otherwise not have done so to join the company.

Unfortunately, just one month following your transfer to the job in offshore construction that you had wanted for so long, in the course of winning the All-African Football Cup with a company team, you sustained torn ligaments of the right leg and were hospitalized for two weeks and in a cast from the thigh down for an additional six weeks. This made it extremely difficult for you to get out of the office, especially to offshore locations. At the same time, while you were in the hospital, your wife took your daughter out in the speedboat. While watching her mother water ski, Yvonne (your daughter) fell out of the speeding boat and sustained damage to her ears, which left her completely deaf. Despite your conviction that the doctors at the company hospital were nonplussed by your daughter's illness and your repeated requests that she be flown out to specialists in Holland, this was not done until some eight weeks ago. During this time, your daughter showed no signs of improvement that you could see and became morose and silent and refused to eat. Since her return to Holland, she has been seen by four ear, nose, and throat specialists (all expenses paid for by Sunglow); her hearing has begun to improve; and they believe that she will recover completely.

Structured Experience   257

Your wife returned to Holland with the child and is living in a flat close to the hospital (again all expenses are paid by Sunglow). However, prior to her departure, you had several serious quarrels with her because you accused her of having caused the child's accident through her negligence. Since then, you have come to believe that your attitude toward her was caused by your concern for the child, your own accident, problems at work, and overcommitment both at work and at the club. This made you extremely nervous and distraught. You hope that she will accept this explanation—which you have made by letter—that she will return to Dunia, and that your relationship will not suffer; but you have not had a reply from her yet.

The project-engineer job proved to be a little larger than you expected but, by and large, you believe that you have done a very adequate job—particularly given the problems you have faced both at work and at home and the time and energy you have devoted to the sports section, which has proved to be good publicity for Sunglow. You have missed a couple of target dates, but you are not the only project engineer to have done that in your section, and you are the least senior in terms of time spent in the section. Even these two targets might have been met had not, in one case, the materials department let you down over delivery dates, and, in the other case, the planning engineers drawn up a wrong design, which the barge supervisor would not put himself out to rebuild without your constant attendance and liaison with engineering planning.

What you would like to do next year is to attend courses in management skills and in project engineering, so that you can carry out your job in offshore construction even better than this year—particularly since you hope you will not have so many problems to deal with outside of work next year. Overall you have enjoyed the work much better than that in land facilities and see it as a necessary next step in your career if you are to be at all successful in the company and move on to general management posts, which is your ambition.

SUNGLOW INTERVIEW-SKILLS OBSERVER SHEET

Instructions: Check the phrases below that best describe what you observe.

The Manager.

1. Helps the employee to analyze problems.
2. Helps the employee to generate solutions.
3. Acts as a clarifier to the employee.
4. Acts as a summarizer.
5. Contributes suggestions from experience and knowledge.
6. Avoids giving the employee ready-made answers.
7. Does not assume that he has all the relevant information.
8. Indicates that he is listening actively to the employee.
9. Responds to nonverbal cues.
10. Talks more than the employee does.
11. Shows interest in the employee.
12. Paraphrases the employee's comments.
13. Confronts and/or challenges the employee.
14. Collaborates with the employee to define problem areas.
15. Helps plan follow-up and next steps.
16. Defines the contract and time limits.

What were some of the *most* helpful things the manager said or did?

What behaviors seemed *least* helpful?

Other comments:

The Employee
1. Seeks to find a mutual solution.
2. Listens to understand the supervisor's point of view.
3. Asks for relevant information.
4. Indicates to the supervisor that he is listening.
5. Responds to nonverbal cues.
6. Talks more than the supervisor does.
7. Paraphrases or seeks to clarify the supervisor's comments.
8. Confronts or challenges the supervisor.
9. Attempts to define specific problem areas.
10. Agrees to plan follow-up steps.
11. Agrees to contract and time limits.

What were some of the *most* helpful things the employee said or did?

What behaviors seemed *least* helpful?

Other comments:

258. SEX-ROLE ATTITUDES: PERSONAL FEEDBACK

Goals

I. To develop an understanding of the ways in which sex-based attitudes influence and are inferred from communication.

II. To discuss attitudes and prejudices about sexes in a nonthreatening environment.

III. To increase awareness of and provide feedback on one's own attitudes, beliefs, and behaviors in regard to sex differences.

Group Size

Any number of groups of six to ten members each. (A balance of males and females is desirable.)

Time Required

Approximately two to three hours.

Materials

I. An index card containing three male and three female Sex-Role Attitudes Stereotyped Statements for each group.

II. A copy of the Sex-Role Attitudes Descriptors Sheet for each participant.

III. A pencil for each participant.

Physical Setting

A large room in which participants can meet in separate groups or a number of small rooms.

Process

I. The facilitator introduces the experience as an exploration of sexual attitudes. He divides the participants into groups of six to ten members each (an equal number of males and females in each group is preferable).

II. The facilitator distributes to each group an index card on which are printed three male and three female Sex-Role Attitudes Stereotyped Statements (the statements for each group may or may not be the same, depending on how much controversy the facilitator wishes to introduce). He tells the members that for each stereotyped statement they are to:

1. Discuss how and why the stereotype may have developed;
2. By consensus, take an affirmative or negative position on each statement; and
3. As a group, develop either supporting or negating arguments to be presented later to the entire group.

He allows the groups one hour to complete these tasks.

III. The facilitator calls time and reconvenes the large group. He directs each group, in turn, to present arguments for or against each stereotyped statement. (Five to ten minutes per group.)

IV. The entire group reacts to and discusses the small groups' arguments about the stereotyped statements.

V. After the group discussion, the facilitator directs the participants to re-form in their original small groups. He distributes a copy of the Sex-Role Attitudes Descriptors Sheet and a pencil to each participant and tells the participants to read the sheet.

VI. After a few minutes, the facilitator instructs the group members to begin the task of listing the names of other members of their small groups as instructed on the Sex-Role Attitudes Descriptors Sheet. He stresses that the descriptors should reflect the image that each other person has projected during the earlier group discussions. The facilitator tells the members that they will have ten to fifteen minutes in which to complete this task.

VII. Members are then instructed to share their lists with the other members of their group and to discuss, if asked, their reasons for each selection. This can be done by having one small-group member receive feedback from the others and then rotating the focus so that all members receive feedback in turn.

VIII. The facilitator then leads the total group in a discussion of the members' learnings from the experience, the feelings they had about being described by others, how the experience affected their sex-role attitudes, and what changes or differences might occur in their communication behavior in the future.

Variations

I. Individuals can choose descriptors that they think apply to themselves, record them for future reference, and check them later against the listings made in the small groups.

II. Before the discussions, members can take the Bem Sex-Role Inventory.[1] Androgyny scores can be calculated after the activity is completed. Relationships between Bem scores and Sex-Role Attitudes Descriptors assigned to individuals are then discussed.

III. Participants can reverse male and female statements to see if they apply to the other sex as well.

IV. All-male and all-female groups can be formed. Each group is given statements about the other sex.

V. Members of male-female dyads can complete the list for each other, exchange and clarify lists, and provide additional feedback for each other.

Similar Structured Experiences: *Vol. III:* Structured Experience **62;** *'73 Annual:* **95;** *Vol. V:* **170;** *'76 Annual:* **184;** *Vol. VI:* **213, 215;** *Vol. VII:* **248, 249, 268.**

Suggested Instruments: *Vol. III:* "Polarization: Opinionnaire on Womanhood"; *'73 Annual:* "Sex-Role Stereotyping Rating Scale"; *'77 Annual:* "Bem Sex-Role Inventory (BSRI)"; *'79 Annual:* "Women as Managers Scale (WAMS)."

Lecturette Sources: *'75 Annual:* "Giving Feedback: An Interpersonal Skill"; *'76 Annual:* "Assertion Theory"; *'77 Annual:* "Androgyny."

Notes on the Use of "Sex-Role Attitudes":

Submitted by Brian P. Holleran.

[1]*The 1977 Annual Handbook for Group Facilitators*, pp. 83-88.

SEX-ROLE ATTITUDES STEREOTYPED STATEMENTS

Male

1. Men are logical.
2. Men are untidy.
3. Men are brave.
4. Men are egotistical.
5. Men are mechanically inclined.
6. Men are cynical.
7. Men are strong.
8. Men like to gamble.
9. Men are aggressive.
10. Men are sexually driven.
11. Men are competitive.
12. Men are happier when they are not married.
13. Men want to be the breadwinners.
14. Men want women to be submissive.
15. Men are not good losers.
16. Men do not know how to cook.
17. Men are smarter than women.
18. Men need women to take care of them.
19. Men do not appreciate delicate things.

Female

1. Women have intuition.
2. Women are bad drivers.
3. Women are neat and tidy.
4. Women are emotional.
5. Women are creative.
6. Women are vain.
7. Women are sensitive and gentle.
8. Women like to keep house and cook.
9. Women are not usually interested in sex.
10. Women are fragile and delicate.
11. Women are competitive.
12. Women are happier when they are married.
13. Women like to shop and spend money.
14. Women want men to take charge.
15. Women are not as physically active as men.
16. Women are afraid of mice and bugs.
17. Women are smarter than men.
18. Women cannot make decisions.
19. Women are devious.

SEX-ROLE ATTITUDES DESCRIPTORS SHEET

Instructions: Below are twenty-two statements that may describe members of your own group. Next to each statement write the first names only of *two* group members who seem to personify that statement, based on the group's interactions. On many statements, for each person chosen, you must also indicate whether you think the statement applies to males or females. Do this by putting each person's first initial next to the male or female designation, e.g., "thinks that males/females . . ." Do *not* include yourself as one of the two people selected for each item.

All statements will complete the following phrase:
"The verbal and nonverbal communication behaviors exhibited by this person seem to indicate that he/she . . ."

1. thinks that males/females should be submissive.   _____ _____

2. thinks that males/females should be aggressive.   _____ _____

3. thinks that there should be equality between the sexes.   _____ _____

4. thinks that males/females should be happy pleasing the other sex.   _____ _____

5. thinks that there should be a sexual double standard.   _____ _____

6. thinks that there is nothing wrong with sexual chauvinism.   _____ _____

7. is verbally denouncing the very behaviors of which he/she is a prime example.   _____ _____

8. is unconvinced that there is any need to discuss sex differences.   _____ _____

9. is well aware of the prejudices that have resulted from sexual stereotyping.   _____ _____

10. really likes the practice of dividing behaviors and experiences according to sex.   _____ _____

11. is aware that current sexual discrimination has prohibited members of one or both sexes from participating in certain positive experiences.   _____ _____

12. is truly an androgynous person.   _____ _____

13. is offended when someone exhibits a behavior typically attributed to the other sex.   _____ _____

14. listens to and cares about what members of the other sex say.   _____ _____

15. is aware of the many behaviors that can be considered insulting to members of the other sex, i.e., a pinch, physical comparisons, etc.   _____ _____

16. values his/her sexual freedom.   _____ _____

17. sees little basis or support for the contention that there is any real sexual discrimination.   _____ _____

18. thinks that a healthy relationship can develop when the sexes are in conflict or competition with each other.   _____ _____

19. thinks that males/females are always looking for persons with whom to share sexual intimacies.   _____ _____

20. sees members of the other sex as helpless.   _____ _____

21. enjoys defending sex differences.   _____ _____

22. is always seeking to reduce the conflict between the sexes.   _____ _____

259. DHABI FEHRU: AN MBO ACTIVITY

Goals

   I. To examine the process of developing task goals for individuals who are working together on a team project.

   II. To provide participants an opportunity to practice writing objectives as part of a Management by Objectives training session.

   III. To experience the difference between preparing goals for oneself and for others.

Group Size

   One to five groups of six to nine members each (eight per group is ideal).

Time Required

   Three hours.

Materials

   I. A copy of the Dhabi Fehru Guidelines for Writing Specific Objectives for each participant (optional).

   II. A copy of the Dhabi Fehru Background Information Sheet for each participant.

   III. A copy of the Dhabi Fehru Task Sheet for each participant.

   IV. A copy of the Dhabi Fehru Observer Sheet for each observer.

   V. Blank paper and a pencil for each participant.

   VI. Newsprint and a felt-tipped marker for each group.

Physical Setting

   A room in which all groups can work without disturbing each other. Chairs and a table for each group.

Process

I. The facilitator presents a lecturette on Management by Objectives (MBO). (This structured experience can also be used during the last three hours of an all-day MBO workshop.)

II. The facilitator reviews the Dhabi Fehru Guidelines for Writing Specific Objectives (copies may be distributed to participants, if desired).

III. The facilitator announces that consultant teams will be formed to prepare objectives for the various departments of the newly formed government of the kingdom of Dhabi Fehru. He divides the participants into groups and appoints an observer from each group.

IV. The facilitator gives each participant a copy of the Dhabi Fehru Background Information Sheet, a copy of the Dhabi Fehru Task Sheet, blank paper, and a pencil. He also gives each observer a copy of the Dhabi Fehru Observer Sheet. He allows time for the participants to read the information and then he answers any questions.

V. The participants are told that they will have two hours in which to complete the task. They are told that this time *includes* their organization time (the time they will have to form a formal group, determine who their leader is, allocate tasks, etc.). The observer in each group serves as the Dhabi Fehru task coordinator. Questions or problems that the coordinator cannot resolve are to be brought to the attention of the facilitator.

VI. The facilitator gives participants a ten-minute time warning and directs each group to post on newsprint *one* objective in *each* area.

VII. The facilitator stops the activity, reassembles the total group, and leads a discussion comparing the various groups' objectives, using the Dhabi Fehru Guidelines for Writing Specific Objectives. The facilitator avoids discussion of content details, e.g., whether certain assumptions are accurate or incorrect; the only relevant concern is whether or not an objective is properly prepared. The facilitator should accept all factual assertions and assumptions made by advisory team members and should concentrate on whether the objectives written from those assumptions meet the criteria of good objectives.

VIII. If desired, the facilitator can focus the group on the task-organization process. This should be done only after the critique of objectives (step VII) is completed. The task coordinators then report on each team's process.

Variations

I. Development of team-member work objectives can be omitted.

II. The facilitator can introduce an element of intergroup competition by announcing that the objectives will be judged and the best advisory team selected.

III. The task coordinator (observer) can be told that he or she is a native of Dhabi Fehru and is concerned with getting the most out of the advisory team. Depending on how strongly this is put, a degree of intercultural conflict can be introduced.

Similar Structured Experiences: *Vol. II:* Structured Experience **39**; *'74 Annual:* **126**; *Vol. V:* **166**; *'76 Annual:* **178**; *'78 Annual:* **232**.

Suggested Instruments: *Vol. II:* "Force-Field Analysis Inventory"; *Vol. III:* "Group-Behavior Questionnaire"; *'75 Annual:* "Decision-Style Inventory."

Lecturette Sources: *'72 Annual:* "Management by Objectives," "Criteria of Effective Goal-Setting: The SPIRO Model"; *'78 Annual:* "Contracting: A Process and a Tool," "Transactions in the Change Process."

Notes on the Use of "Dhabi Fehru":

Submitted by Dwight Bechtel.

DHABI FEHRU GUIDELINES FOR WRITING SPECIFIC OBJECTIVES

Format for a Well Stated Objective:

1. Person(s) responsible
2. Action verb
3. Specific, measurable end result
4. Specific time period or date
5. Cost in dollars and/or work hours.

A good objective states the *who, what, when,* and *maximum cost* but avoids the *how* and the *feasibility.* The action plan will cover the how and test the feasibility.

Check List for a Good Statement of an Objective

Items 1 through 5 on this check list are critical. Items 6 through 10 are important but not necessarily critical (as part of the written objective).

1. Is the objective stated in explicit and concrete terms? If possible, is it *quantified?*
2. Does it state *what* is to be done?
3. Does it state what the objective hopes to *achieve?*
4. Does it state *who* has responsibility for doing it?
5. Does it state *when* it is to be completed?
6. Does it contain a succinct statement explaining the *approach* to be employed in order to achieve the objective?
7. Does it include a statement of the *justification* for accomplishing the objective?
8. Does it detail the *resources* necessary for its accomplishment?
9. Does it state who is to *coordinate* different parts of the overall objective?
10. Does it state the *criteria* by which the accomplishment of the objective can be measured?

Common Deficiencies in Statements of Objectives

1. Objectives are set too low to truly challenge capabilities.
2. Individuals or groups overestimate their capabilities with inappropriate or impossible objectives.
3. Objectives do not reflect the responsibilities of the individuals who make them.
4. The objective is concerned with *how* to do something rather than with *what* is to be done.
5. No one is assigned responsibility for achieving the objective.
6. Objectives reflect an individual's perception of what the boss wants, not what can actually be achieved.
7. Objectives that are subsequently proven unfeasible, irrelevant, or impossible are not revised or deleted.

8. Objective completion dates are too optimistic.
9. The justification for an objective is not clearly stated.
10. The approach designed to achieve the objective is inadequate.

Examples of Well Stated Objectives

1. The mail-room supervisor will be responsible for providing mail pickup from and distribution to five central locations within the company three times daily so as to maximize convenience for all fifteen departments. This objective shall be accomplished by January 15 at an implementation cost of no more than $550 and twenty hours work time, with an increased operational cost to the mail room not to exceed $100 and five work hours per week.

2. The head of the maintenance department and the assistant manager of computer operations will act as a team to be responsible for developing and implementing a computerized program for building maintenance by October 31 at a cost of no more than $2,000 and forty work hours.

3. The executive team, working with the personnel director, shall take actions to reduce the organizational absentee rate from 9 percent to 5 percent, by September 1, at a cost not to exceed thirty-five work hours and with no increase in the existing budget.

4. The training director will develop a communication-skills program for mid-level managers, costing no more than forty work hours to develop and no more than $500 per manager to operate (including the training department's budget as well as the cost of the manager's time, with a maximum allowable time charge of $300 per manager).

DHABI FEHRU BACKGROUND INFORMATION SHEET

Dhabi Fehru is a small country on the Persian Gulf coast. The population of two million consists primarily of nomadic desert tribespeople who have been ruled for centuries by one of the eight sheiks. In 1880, Dhabi Fehru became a British Protectorate; when this status ended five years ago, the ruler, Emir Ibn Ben Dhab, proclaimed his state an independent nation and was crowned king. Dhabi Fehru is about the size of Colorado, but most of the land area is desert. There are only two cities of any size, Dhabistan (the capital), with a population of 200,000, and Kalmiz, with 70,000 inhabitants.

Since huge oil reserves were discovered about four years ago, there have been some changes, especially in the overall standard of living. Per capita income is among the highest in the world. Food, housing, education, and medical services are free to all citizens (within the limits set by availability—there is, for example, one hospital in the country). Five years ago the literacy rate was close to zero; now it is about 10 percent. English is a second language to most of the population—a heritage of British rule.

Oil income is expected to rise for at least the next decade. After that, it should be stable for at least another ten years before beginning to decline slowly as the oil reserves are depleted. The king has, therefore, decided to mount an all-out effort toward creating for Dhabi Fehru a self-sustaining industrial base. Toward this aim, King Dhab has recently brought in several teams of Western advisors to create specific objectives for development.

DHABI FEHRU TASK SHEET

Dhabi Fehru has immense wealth; per capita income is among the highest of any nation in the world. The oil will not, however, last forever. The ruler, King Ibn Ben Dhab has brought in several consultant teams to advise him in his effort to develop Dhabi Fehru into a modern industrial nation. You are a member of one of these teams.

Your group's observer will serve as task coordinator. He or she is to assist your group of advisors to whatever extent is deemed appropriate. The task coordinator is to record team organization (who the team leader is, etc.). A formal organizational chart is required. Teams not submitting an organizational chart showing each member's formal position will be dismissed and sent home on the next freighter.

Once the advisory team has determined its formal structure, each consultant will prepare objectives for one or more of the areas listed below. Prior to beginning this task, written objectives must be given to the task coordinator.

Persons who hold supervisory positions in the advisory team (not including the task coordinator) may not work on developing objectives for Dhabi Fehru but may advise subordinates, as appropriate. Supervisors may consult with their subordinates in developing the subordinates' work objectives.

Consultants—advisory team members other than supervisors—will prepare objectives for one or more of the following areas:

Education	Foreign Affairs
Health	Recreation
Armed Forces	Welfare
Industry	Transportation
Water and Sewage	Energy
Housing	Environmental Protection
Agriculture	Finance and Investments

Each of these areas *must* be assigned and covered.

Task Summary

1. Organize; provide task coordinator with a team organizational chart.
2. Prepare work objectives for each advisory team member.
3. Prepare objectives for Dhabi Fehru.

You have two hours in which to complete these tasks.

DHABI FEHRU OBSERVER SHEET

1. You are to approve or disapprove your group's organizational chart. All members of the advisory team must be shown on the chart. You may not make suggestions on how to make the chart. The chart need not follow traditional organizational patterns. As long as everyone is assigned a position within the organization, it is acceptable.

2. Observe to see if there are any specific skill considerations in assigning jobs during the activity.

3. Enforce the writing of work objectives before allowing advisors to begin writing objectives for Dhabi Fehru.

4. Check all work objectives to see if each contains the following:
   a. Person(s) responsible
   b. Action verb
   c. Specific, measurable end result
   d. Specific time period or date
   e. Cost in dollars and/or work hours.

   Question the group members to be sure that they understand the task, i.e., do all members thoroughly understand the objective in its final form?

5. You may answer questions as you see fit. While you need not share the information on this sheet, you may choose to do so. In order for the project to go well, you must share the information on the Dhabi Fehru Task Sheet and you must carry out the above instructions.

260. ISLAND COMMISSION: GROUP PROBLEM SOLVING

Goals

I. To experience the issues involved in long-range social planning.

II. To study emergent group dynamics and leadership in the completion of a group task.

III. To explore aspects of communication, problem solving, and decision making in a work group.

Group Size

An unlimited number of groups of eight members each.

Time Required

Two to two and one-half hours.

Materials

I. A copy of the Island Commission Task Agenda Sheet and a copy of the Island Commission Major City Information Sheet for each participant.

II. One copy each of Island Commission Environmental Bulletins 1, 2, and 3 for each participant.

III. A place card with a role name (these may be made by folding 5″ x 8″ index cards in half lengthwise and writing role names on them with a felt-tipped marker) for each participant.

IV. A pencil for each participant.

V. Newsprint and a felt-tipped marker for each group.

Physical Setting

A room large enough that all groups can meet separately without disturbing one another and eight chairs and a table for each group.

Process

I. The facilitator divides the participants into groups of eight members each and gives each member a copy of the Island Commission Task Agenda Sheet, a copy of the Island Commission Major City Information Sheet, and a pencil. He designates each member of the group to play one of the following roles:

1. director of city planning
2. director of community action council
3. director of chamber of commerce
4. general manager of food-processing factory (largest industry in Major City)
5. organization development consultant
6. council member, farmer
7. council member, dentist
8. council member, lawyer.

He gives each member an appropriate name place card.

II. Participants are told that they have one hour in which to conduct the four meetings outlined on the Island Commission Task Agenda Sheet and to list their recommendations on newsprint. Groups then are directed to their meeting areas.

III. While they are meeting, the facilitator announces each fifteen-minute interval and tells the groups that each fifteen-minute period corresponds with a new three-month meeting of the commission. Before the second meeting he distributes Island Commission Environmental Bulletin 1; before the third meeting he distributes Island Commission Environmental Bulletin 2; and before the last meeting he distributes Island Commission Environmental Bulletin 3.

IV. At the conclusion of the meetings, the facilitator assembles the entire group and requests a progress report and set of recommendations from each commission group. He posts the recommendations from each group.

V. The facilitator solicits comments about the feelings and frustrations of members during the group meetings. He may ask the following questions:

1. What roles tended to assume leadership and/or tried to control the group process?
2. What hidden agendas were operating?
3. How did new data affect the problem-solving process?
4. How did the roles affect communication in the groups?
5. How were decisions made? How was this affected by the composition, structure, and task of the group?

He then leads the group in a discussion of the difficulties inherent in long-range planning. He may focus on the problems of data changes (learning based on the past may not be applicable to the future), specialization (increasing professionalism and social differentiation), a decrease in physical resources, uncertain social resources (i.e., social stability), and an increasing rate of change coupled with less decision-making time.

Variations

I. The consultant can give process feedback after the first and third meetings.

II. Groups can be set up to compete with each other. The group with the "best" set of recommendations is "awarded" the grant.

III. Roles can be switched for one of the meetings.

Similar Structured Experiences: *Vol. I:* Structured Experience **9;** *Vol. III:* **69;** *Vol. IV:* **102;** *'74 Annual:* **134;** *'77 Annual:* **192;** *Vol. VII:* **259.**

Suggested Instruments: *Vol. II:* "Force-Field Analysis Inventory"; *'78 Annual:* "Phases of Integrated Problem Solving (PIPS)."

Lecturette Sources: *'73 Annual:* "Kurt Lewin's 'Force Field Analysis'"; *'74 Annual:* "Hidden Agendas"; *'75 Annual:* "Common Problems in Volunteer Groups"; *'77 Annual:* "Constructive Citizen Participation"; *'79 Annual:* "Finishing Unfinished Business: Creative Problem Solving."

Notes on the Use of "Island Commission":

Submitted by Peter G. Gillan.

ISLAND COMMISSION TASK AGENDA SHEET

Background

You have been recruited by the mayor of Major City to be a member of a special commission. You accepted enthusiastically, since you want to have an impact on the important long-range recommendations that the commission will develop. You are widely respected on the island and are known to be an expert in your specialty. The mayor has indicated that your frame of reference will be important to the commission's functioning.

The Job of the Commission

The commission was formed as one of the requirements for getting a large grant for Major City. A total of twenty million dollars has been earmarked for the city—four million a year for five years.

The mayor has formed the commission to:

1. Formulate a plan for consideration of the important factors affecting the city's future; and
2. Make specific recommendations to the Major City Governmental Council for the use of the funds.

The funds will begin arriving in eighteen months, and the mayor has given the commission twelve months to complete its work. The mayor has explained that he formed this blue-ribbon commission so that the recommendations would have the greatest possible weight and that he will work for the adoption of all the commission's recommendations.

One important background factor is that no more than 50 percent of the funds may go into capital development; i.e., human service programs must comprise at least one-half of the commission's recommendations.

The Meeting Schedule

The next hour represents the four major quarterly meetings of the commission. Each meeting will last about fifteen minutes in "real time."

1. At the first meeting, the assignment is to create a "chart of work" for the commission's next three meetings.
2. The second and third meetings are for carrying out the chart of work.
3. A product of the last meeting will be an actual set of recommendations for the use of the twenty million dollars over the next five years. (You also will be asked to hand in this list on a sheet of newsprint.)

Note: Take a minute to get into the feeling of your role. Imagine what a person in your role would think. What viewpoints would you hold? What would be important to you as you act out your role? Having thought about these things, behave from this frame of reference as you participate in the commission meetings.

ISLAND COMMISSION MAJOR CITY INFORMATION SHEET

Major City is located on the coast of Independent Island (250 square miles), two hundred miles from the mainland of Friendly Power.

The population of 200,000 has grown rapidly in recent years because of immigration.

These are forty square miles of city and suburbs. The surrounding area is good agricultural land. Little unused land remains in the urban area.

All power for domestic and industrial use depends on fuel imported from Friendly Power. The present power plant is being operated at 98 percent of capacity. The sewer and water plants are now operating beyond design capacity.

Major City's economy depends on the processing and export of the agricultural production of the island (35 percent), minerals mined on the island (15 percent), tourism (25 percent), the Friendly Power naval base (10 percent), and miscellaneous income (15 percent). Although the general economy is good, there is some unemployment and a sizable population of poor people.

Half of Major City's food is grown on the island. In addition to the beaches and climate, the major attractions are the island's unspoiled rural scene and the fresh fruits and vegetables, available all year, that are the basis of the famous native cuisine.

The airport, located on the navy base, is used jointly for military and commercial planes. The harbor has been famous for centuries. Although picturesque, it is a very busy port, suitable for modern ships.

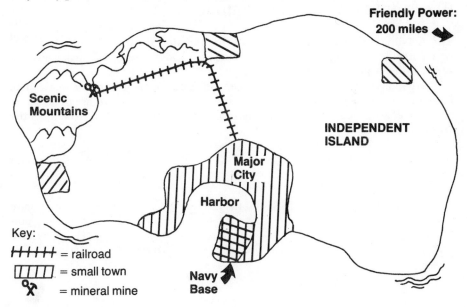

Friendly Power:
200 miles

Scenic Mountains

INDEPENDENT ISLAND

Major City

Harbor

Key:

H++++ = railroad

⊓⊓⊓ = small town

⚒ = mineral mine

Navy Base

ISLAND COMMISSION ENVIRONMENTAL BULLETIN 1

The schools of Major City have become badly overcrowded, and a study just released to the news media states statistical proof that the quality of education is slipping.

The supply of transportation fuel has, without warning, been cut by 50 percent. Reports indicate that this is not a temporary shortage.

The heavy tourist influx from Friendly Power is just beginning, and the car rental people are expecting a big season.

ISLAND COMMISSION ENVIRONMENTAL BULLETIN 2

Growth in Major City has resulted in the need to expand the hospital facilities. The food-processing industry on which the city depends heavily also needs to expand in order to survive. The hospital and the industry are competing for the same space; no other space is available within the city limits.

The Friendly Power Navy has recently learned and has proof that a large part of the economy of Independent Island has depended on the illicit cultivation of opium poppies. The Navy has stated that if the traffic in opium is not eliminated, it will pull out of its installation.

ISLAND COMMISSION ENVIRONMENTAL BULLETIN 3

The Aviation Administration has stated that the airport cannot handle the large transport and passenger jets now in almost exclusive use by all major airlines serving the island.

Organized low-income residents demand that no expenditures be made until housing for the poor is provided. The older, established residents are demanding two-acre zoning for all new housing starts, in order to preserve the character of the city and the island.

261. WANTS BOMBARDMENT: A PSYCHOSYNTHESIS ACTIVITY

Goals

I. To increase awareness of competing wants in one's life situation.

II. To attempt to prioritize and/or synthesize one's wants.

Group Size

An unlimited number of groups of seven members each.

Time Required

Approximately one and one-half hours.

Materials

Two sheets of paper and a pencil for each participant.

Physical Setting

A room large enough for the groups to engage in rather noisy interaction without disturbing each other. Participants should be able to sit comfortably on the floor.

Process

I. The facilitator briefly discusses the goals of the activity, explaining how needs and wants differ.

II. The facilitator distributes the paper and pencils and instructs the participants to "brainstorm" all their wants. Each participant is to list a large quantity of things, experiences, opportunities, etc., that he or she wants right now. The facilitator says that although participants may think that some wants are not "realistic," they are not to censor their lists. (Five minutes.)

III. Each participant is told to select six particularly appealing wants from his list and to write them on a new piece of paper. Beside each of the six, participants are to write notes to themselves about how they are experiencing the want (how they think, feel, behave, etc., when they are wanting it). (Five minutes.)

IV. The facilitator forms groups of seven members each by any convenient method. Groups are separated from each other and are seated in circles (preferably on the floor).

V. The facilitator explains the following sequence, which will be carried out for each of the seven members of each group:

1. A member volunteers to be "it."
2. "It" sits in the center of the circle; the other members close the circle around that person.
3. The person who is "it" assigns one want to each of the other members and explains some of the quality of that want from the notes he made on experiencing that want.
4. With his eyes closed, "it" is bombarded by the six wants: the others talk *simultaneously* as if they were the want, incorporating the quality of the want for that person, e.g., "I want to lose weight, I want to go on a diet, I want to reduce, I want to lose weight, I want to be slimmer, etc." "I want to have more friends, I want to develop more friendships, I want to have more close friends, I want to be friends with more people, etc."

   The other members simply *paraphrase* the want repeatedly. The person being "it" can shift about so as to avoid any one want being spoken directly into the ear.
5. When "it" achieves a sense of insight or "closure," he stops the process by raising his arms. "It" remains quiet, with his eyes closed, for a few seconds to crystallize his reactions to the bombardment. Then these reactions and insights are shared with the group. (Two to three minutes.)
6. The group *briefly* discusses possible action implications for "it." The facilitator then answers any procedural questions.

   (It is often helpful at this point for the facilitator to demonstrate the sequence, using his or her own wants.)

VI. Groups go through the sequence seven times. The facilitator monitors the groups, responds to procedural questions, and makes suggestions to ensure that the wants compete "fairly" with each other within each group.

VII. The facilitator leads a discussion of the entire experience, drawing out contributions from individuals. The following open-ended sentences can serve as a guide for this sharing:

1. What I learned about my wants was . . .
2. What I relearned about my wants was . . .
3. What I am beginning to learn about my wants is . . .
4. What I am going to do about my wants is . . .

Variations

I. Individuals who do not wish to participate can function as observers and/or as coaches in the process.

II. Any individual can be permitted to repeat the sequence, with either different persons representing his or her wants or with different wants.

III. In an intact group or a group with some history, "it" can provide feedback to the other members by explaining why he chose each of them to represent a particular want.

Similar Structured Experiences: *Vol. III:* Structured Experience **65;** *'74 Annual:* **128, 129;** *'75 Annual:* **137, 143;** *'76 Annual:* **182.**

Suggested Instrument: *'79 Annual:* "Satisfaction Survey: An Affective Personal Feedback Instrument."

Lecturette Sources: *'72 Annual:* "The Maslow Need Hierarchy"; *'74 Annual:* "Figure/Ground"; *'75 Annual:* "Human Needs and Behavior," "What is Psychosynthesis?"; *'76 Annual:* "The Awareness Wheel."

Notes on the Use of "Wants Bombardment":

This activity is in general use in the practice of psychosynthesis; its origin is unknown. This version was written by John E. Jones.

262. PHYSICAL CHARACTERISTICS: DYADIC PERCEPTION CHECKING

Goals

I. To examine one's reactions to the physical characteristics of others.

II. To learn to observe others more accurately.

III. To study the effects of generalizing and stereotyping.

Group Size

Unlimited.

Time Required

Forty-five minutes to one hour.

Materials

I. A copy of the Physical Characteristics Description Sheet for each participant.

II. A pencil for each participant.

Physical Setting

A room large enough for the dyads to be seated apart from each other and a writing surface for each participant.

Process

I. The facilitator instructs the participants to form dyads (pairs) with persons they do not know.

II. The facilitator distributes a copy of the Physical Characteristics Description Sheet and a pencil to each participant.

III. He instructs each participant to learn his partner's name and then to sit in silence for five minutes while making observations about the other person and recording them on the Physical Characteristics Description Sheet.

IV. Participants are instructed to confirm any information they could not obtain by silent observation. (Five minutes.)

V. Participants then turn over the Physical Characteristics Description Sheet and write a *brief* essay on the meaning of the other person's physical characteristics. The essay should focus on the different meanings of permanent, genetically determined characteristics as well as those that relate to nutrition and other personal habits. (Ten minutes.)

VI. The members of each dyad exchange descriptions. Each partner verbally "corrects" the description of himself, including inaccuracies in the physical description as well as the content of the essay. (Five minutes.)

VII. Each participant shares what he inferred about his partner *from what the partner said or left unsaid in his essay description*. Participants then share past experiences of having their physical characteristics misinterpreted. (Fifteen minutes.)

VIII. The facilitator assembles the entire group and leads a discussion of the feelings and the learnings generated by the experience. He may ask the following questions:

1. How does it feel to have your physical characteristics scrutinized?
2. How does it feel to focus on another person's physical characteristics?
3. How accurate were your observations?
4. What is the difference between describing characteristics and attributing meaning to them?
5. What stereotypes or generalizations surfaced? Had they been experienced before?
6. What effects do these generalizations have on attraction to and communication with others?
7. What might be done to prevent stereotypes from interfering with the getting-acquainted process?

Variations

I. The entire experience can be done with written exchanges.

II. The description sheet can be filled out as an interview.

III. The experience can focus on male/female, racial, or other specific issues.

IV. Participants can be instructed to draw caricatures of themselves or each other, based on the essays.

Similar Structured Experiences: *Vol. II:* Structured Experience 42; *Vol. III:* **50, 58, 63;** *'73 Annual:* **88;** *Vol. V:* **170;** *'76 Annual:* **174, 180;** *Vol. VI:* **213;** *'78 Annual:* **227.**

Suggested Instruments: *'72 Annual:* "Interpersonal Relationship Rating Scale"; *'77 Annual:* "Interpersonal Check List (ICL)."

Lecturette Sources: *'72 Annual:* "Assumptions About the Nature of Man"; *'73 Annual:* "Thinking and Feeling"; *'76 Annual:* "Interpersonal Feedback as Consensual Validation of Constructs."

Notes on the Use of "Physical Characteristics":

Submitted by Allen J. Schuh.

PHYSICAL CHARACTERISTICS DESCRIPTION SHEET

Instructions: Check or circle those descriptions that apply to your partner. Make any notes that you think are pertinent.

First name of person described: _____

1. Hair (color, length, curly or straight, widow's peak, style)
2. Facial hair (whiskers, beard, mustache, sideburns)
3. Eyebrows (straight, arched, thick, thin, plucked)
4. Eyes (color, shape, spacing)
5. Eyeglasses, contact lenses, or sunglasses
6. Evidence of need for glasses (squinting, peering, etc.)
7. Chin (normal, protruding, receding)
8. Nose (large, small, crooked, straight, broad, thin)
9. Mouth (full, thin, sensuous, cruel, open, closed, color)
10. Teeth (condition, size, color)
11. Ears (large, small, protruding, flat, size of lobes)
12. Neck (thick, thin, long, short)
13. Race (black, white, Oriental, etc.)
14. Skin (color, texture, scars or marks, tattoos)
15. Hands (condition of fingers, bent or straight, hairiness)
16. Fingernails (length, condition, cleanliness)
17. Feet (small, large, type of shoe)
18. Body build (heavy, thin, muscular, average, shapely, etc.)
19. Height (normal, tall, short)
20. Weight (average, over, under)
21. Evidence of illness or allergies
22. Age
23. Clothing:

cap or hat	undershirt	socks, hose
jacket or coat	shirt or blouse or T-shirt	jewelry or watch
bra	dress or trousers	cosmetics
slip	shoes	perfume or scent

24. Unique characteristics
25. General cleanliness

Name of person providing description: _____

Structured Experience   262

263. TRADING CARDS: A POWER SIMULATION

Goals

I. To experience the consequences of conflict between group goals and goals of individual members.

II. To experience intergroup and intragroup competition.

III. To identify patterns of competition and cooperation among group members in a stressful situation.

IV. To identify how group and individual strategies affect the group's attainment of a goal.

Group Size

Ten to twenty-eight participants in two to four equal-sized groups of at least five members each.

Time Required

One and one-half to two hours.

Materials

I. A copy of the Trading Cards Rule Sheet for each participant.

II. A copy of the Trading Cards Score Sheet for each group.

III. One set of five Trading Cards (one yellow, one green, one pink, one blue, and one white) in a large envelope for each participant. (Index cards or equal-sized pieces of colored construction paper can be used.)

IV. A name tag containing a name or a geometric (group) symbol for each member of each group. (Each group's name or symbol is different from those of the other groups.)

V. Newsprint and a felt-tipped marker.

Physical Setting

A large, open area, allowing free movement of all participants.

Process

I. The facilitator tells the participants that structured experiences can be used to evoke real responses to simulated situations. He encourages them to focus their awareness on their behaviors and feelings in the forthcoming experience.

II. Participants are arbitrarily divided into two to four equal groups of at least five persons each. Each member is given a large envelope containing five Trading Cards (one yellow, one green, one pink, one blue, and one white) and a name tag containing the name or symbol of his group. Members are instructed to wear their tags on their chests.

III. The facilitator then gives each participant a copy of the Trading Cards Rule Sheet. He goes over the rules and explains that there are two kinds of winner, an individual winner and a group winner. The individual winner is the person or persons whose cards have the highest point value at the end of the final round of play. The group with the highest total of individual scores at the end of the final round of play is the group winner.

IV. The facilitator gives a copy of the Trading Cards Score Sheet to each group. (He does *not* point out that all participants can finish equally with the same cards they started with, i.e., they do not have to trade.)

V. The facilitator announces the beginning of the first of six rounds of trading. (Five minutes.)

VI. At the end of the round, the facilitator announces a five-minute scoring period.

VII. Five more rounds are conducted, with a scoring period after each round. After the scoring of rounds 2 and 3, the facilitator announces that the teams have five minutes in which to discuss their strategies for the next round. After the scoring period for round 4, he announces that groups *may* consult with each other for five minutes if they wish to do so.

VIII. At the end of the final round, the teams' final totals are tabulated. Each team reports its total score, its individual high score, and the name of the team's individual winner. These are listed on newsprint by the facilitator.

IX. The facilitator gives a lecturette on power and competition and their impact on team functioning (fifteen minutes). He then directs the participants to discuss how they feel about having participated in the experience. The participants then discuss their strategies and styles of interaction, including which behaviors (cooperative or competitive) got them what they wanted, which behaviors did not, and what effect this had on the groups. The facilitator asks the participants how they decided who they would trade with and what they would trade. After the discussion, learnings from the experience are summarized and applied to other situations.

Variations

I. The facilitator can control the tempo of trading by introducing new information and/or rules before the commencement of each round. For example, individual competition can be heightened by announcing individual scores and emphasizing changes in individual standings.

II. Participants can be instructed to trade (a) only within their group, (b) only outside their group, and (c) both within and outside of their group.

Similar Structured Experiences: *Vol. I:* Structured Experience 7; *Vol. II:* **35, 36;** *Vol. III:* **61;** *'72 Annual:* **78, 83;** *'75 Annual:* **147;** *Vol. V:* **164, 167;** *'76 Annual:* **179;** *'77 Annual:* **189;** *Vol. VI:* **205;** *'78 Annual:* **231;** *Vol. VII:* **264.**

Suggested Instruments: *'74 Annual:* "Reactions to Group Situations Test"; *'77 Annual:* "TORI Group Self-Diagnosis Scale"; *'78 Annual:* "Mach V Attitude Inventory"; *'79 Annual:* "Power and OD Intervention Analysis (PODIA)."

Lecturette Sources: *'73 Annual:* "Win/Lose Situations"; *'74 Annual:* "Conflict-Resolution Strategies"; *'76 Annual:* "Power."

Notes on the Use of "Trading Cards":

Submitted by Jay Proescher. Based on and adapted from *Starpower*, by R. Garry Shirts. *Starpower* simulation kits are available from NTL/Learning Resources Corporation, 7594 Eads Avenue, La Jolla, CA 92037.

TRADING CARDS RULE SHEET

Each round of trading is governed by the following rules:

1. Each trading round lasts five minutes.
2. Participants who wish to bargain must hold hands.
3. There is absolutely no talking except while holding hands.
4. Once players join hands, a legal trade must be made; i.e., two cards of different color must be swapped.
5. Only one-card-for-one-card transactions are legal.
6. A player may indicate that he chooses not to trade by folding his arms across his chest.
7. A player may not show his cards to anyone, with the exception of the one card he is trading to another player.

Scoring: At the end of each round, each team gathers to calculate its individual and team scores. The score is the total number of points for the cards actually held by each player.

Yellow Card:	50 points
Green Card:	25 points
Pink Card:	15 points
Blue Card:	10 points
White Card:	5 points

In addition, bonus points are awarded for holding three or more cards of the same color.

Three cards of same color:	10 points
Four cards of same color:	20 points
Five cards of same color:	30 points

For example, the score of a hand of three blue cards and two yellow cards is 140 points:

3 blues @ 10:	30
2 yellows @ 50:	100
Bonus:	10
	140

TRADING CARDS SCORE SHEET

Group Symbol: _____

Individual Members	Rounds					
	I	II	III	IV	V	VI
1						
2						
3						
4						
5						
Totals						

264. WAR GAMING: AN INTERGROUP COMPETITION

Goals

I. To study group decision making and interaction under stress.

II. To examine the importance of cooperation in small-group work.

III. To demonstrate the effects of win-win and win-lose approaches to inter-group conflict.

Group Size

Three groups of about six members each.

Time Required

Two to four hours.

Materials

I. A War Gaming Preliminary Instruction Sheet for each team. (Each team receives either a square, circle, or triangle designation, marked by the facilitator ahead of time.)

II. At least three copies of the War Gaming Grid Map for each team. (These can be prepared most easily on graph paper.)

III. A War Gaming Conflict Instruction Sheet for each participant.

IV. Blank paper and a pencil for each participant.

Physical Setting

A room in which the groups can meet without overhearing one another.

Process

I. The facilitator explains to the participants that they will be participating in an intergroup-conflict situation in which they will take the offensive only and that the element of chance has been minimized so that skill will determine success.

117

II. The facilitator randomly selects three people to be "captains." Each captain picks one other person to be on his team. The criterion for selection should be that the people believe they can work well together under stress. Each pair then discusses who the third team member should be and selects that person. The selection process continues until all participants have been placed on teams. (Five to ten minutes.)

III. Each team receives a War Gaming Preliminary Instruction Sheet containing a square, a circle, and a triangle, one of which will be indicated as each team's symbol. Each member receives blank paper and a pencil. The facilitator goes over the instructions with the participants and tells them that they will have fifteen minutes for this phase of the activity. He also announces that each team is to be referred to by its symbol from this point on.

IV. The facilitator gives each team a copy of the War Gaming Grid Map and demonstrates how troops and equipment are deployed. He explains that the three teams are armies and that they are engaged in a three-way conflict. Each team's objective is to have more remaining of its army at the end of the hostilities than any other team—any advantage in force can result in victory.

V. The facilitator distributes the War Gaming Conflict Instruction Sheet to all participants and goes over the instructions with them.

VI. He then directs the teams to position themselves, one in each of three corners of the room. (The fourth corner is designated neutral territory for prisoners.) He says that each team has ten minutes in which to deploy its resources secretly in the block marked "Our Army" on its War Gaming Grid Map.

VII. The facilitator then announces that the teams have five minutes in which to plan their strategies before the commencement of hostilities. He says that if a team uses more time to prepare, another team may attack it first. He reminds the teams that when they are deciding how to deploy their firepower and who they will attack first, they should consider making the team they see as the greatest threat their initial victim, in order to reduce that team's strength. The facilitator says that he will call time at the end of the five-minute planning period, and that any team can begin the conflict by identifying its victim and calling out its first three shots. The teams will then take turns in clockwise rotation.

VIII. The activity continues until any team sustains direct hits on five pieces of equipment or units, at which time that team must surrender one team member to the neutral ground. Prisoners are allowed to talk to each other, but they may not communicate with their former team members.

IX. The activity continues until one team is annihilated, either by loss of equipment and units or by loss of team members. (Approximately thirty minutes.) At that point, all activity stops and the team with the most pieces remaining is declared the victor. That team's symbol is displayed and its anthem (created in step III) is sung by all participants.

X. The facilitator announces that the participants now have the option of engaging in another round of conflict with fresh armaments or of declaring a truce and processing the activity. Teams are given five minutes to make their decisions. All teams must agree before a truce can be declared. (If the conflict is continued, the two teams that appear weaker frequently join forces or collude to vanquish the stronger team. One of the collaborating teams may then "double-cross" the other. These strategies are allowed, although they are not suggested by the facilitator.)

XI. If the conflict is to continue, the prisoners are reassigned to teams in the following way: the winning team is first to select one member, the runner-up team has second choice, and the vanquished team is last to select a member. The selection process rotates until all prisoners are reassigned.

XII. The facilitator distributes another copy of the War Gaming Grid Map and declares that "to the victor belong the spoils." He says that the victorious team will gain (and draw in) one additional row and column (K and 11) on its grid map. The runner-up gains or loses nothing, and the vanquished team loses one row and column (J and 10).

XIII. The conflict begins with the deployment of resources (see step VI) and continues until the completion of the battle or until all three teams agree to a peace treaty or truce.

XIV. The total group is assembled, and the facilitator leads the participants in a discussion of the experience. Some of the following may be considered:
   1. Which team won? What is the nature and effect of "winning"?
   2. Which team lost? What is the nature and effect of "losing"? .
   3. What were the feelings of those team members assigned to prisoner status? How did their reactions affect future team functioning?
   4. How did teams participate in the conflict? What was the level of involvement in winning?
   5. What leadership patterns emerged? What were the characteristics of the leaders? How did these compare to the leadership positions of the captains?
   6. How did teams plan their use of resources? What effects did this have on the results of the battle?
   7. What strategies were employed? What effect did these have on morale?
   8. What alternatives to winning or losing were considered? What risks were taken by each team? How were probabilities examined?

Structured Experience 264

XV. Team members are encouraged to relate what they learned about intra- and intergroup cooperation and conflict, win-lose situations, and negotiation and how these relate to their back-home situations and to conflict in general.

Variations

I. The number of rounds can be fixed and a variable number of shots per round allowed. For example, in the first two rounds, each team can take six shots; in the next two rounds, each team can take five shots, etc.

II. The facilitator can announce several conditions without prior warning:
1. After the attack commences, the facilitator calls out ten random grid positions as "mines." Mines have no allies and explode on each team's map.
2. An "air strike" by an unknown aggressor eliminates one entire alphabetical row on each team's map.
3. "Plague" eliminates half the remaining infantry on each team's map.
4. "Weather" eliminates the tanks on each team's map.

III. The facilitator can randomly select a time to call up "reserves." When the reserves are called up, all unhit elements on the grid map double. Thus, an unhit tank yields another tank that can be positioned anywhere on the grid map that has unhit room for it.

IV. The facilitator can conduct another activity such as "Circle in the Square" or "Win as Much as You Can"[1] to check on what the participants learned about competition and cooperation.

V. Victory conditions can be specified. "Decisive" victory is when two teams are completely eliminated in the final move of the cycle. "Tactical" victory is when one team is eliminated. "Marginal" victory is when the cycle terminates by mutual agreement without a total loss to one of the teams.

VI. One of the team's own occupied grid-map positions must be exposed each round. The other teams may or may not elect to shoot at the elements. Usually, teams assume that infantry positions only are exposed. If the round ends without an exposed position being hit, it counts the same as any other unhit element.

VII. As part of step X, teams also can elect to negotiate (about exchanging team members, declaring a truce, and so on). A halt to hostilities can be called only if all three teams agree. The truce lasts as long as the captains wish to

---

[1]Structured Experiences 36 (*Handbook*, Volume II) and 205 (*Handbook*, Volume VI). See "Similar Structured Experiences" at the end of this structured experience.

discuss issues either with their teams or other captains. The truce can be broken at any time and by anyone. The thirty-second rule for calling shots again comes into effect.

VIII. Total surrender can be allowed. For total surrender, the entire team must agree or the team *members* must agree to revolt unanimously against the captain, who then is sent to the neutral corner. The team members then relinquish their turn to the captain of whichever team offers them the best terms.

Similar Structured Experiences: *Vol. II:* Structured Experiences **35, 36;** *Vol. III:* **61;** *'72 Annual:* **78, 83;** *Vol. IV:* **124;** *'75 Annual:* **145, 147;** *Vol. V:* **164;** *'76 Annual:* **179;** *'77 Annual:* **189;** *Vol. VI:* **205;** *'78 Annual:* **231;** *Vol. VII:* **263, 265.**

Suggested Instruments: *Vol. III:* "Group-Climate Inventory," "Group-Growth Evaluation Form"; *'75 Annual:* "Decision-Style Inventory"; *'78 Annual:* "Mach V Attitude Inventory."

Lecturette Sources: *'73 Annual:* "Win/Lose Situations"; *'74 Annual:* "Conflict-Resolution Strategies"; *'76 Annual:* "Power"; *'77 Annual:* "Constructive Conflict in Discussions: Learning to Manage Disagreements Effectively," "Handling Group and Organizational Conflict"; *'78 Annual:* "Tolerance of Equivocality: The Bronco, Easy Rider, Blockbuster, and Nomad."

Notes on the Use of "War Gaming":

Submitted by Allen J. Schuh.

WAR GAMING GRID MAP

Equipment

Two tanks that occupy four square, adjoining grid spaces each:

Two artillery batteries that occupy three adjoining grid spaces each: , , or

Six infantry units that occupy one grid space each: ☐

(These pieces of equipment and units will occupy a total of twenty grid spaces and will remain in the same positions throughout the conflict.)

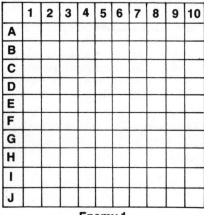

Enemy 1

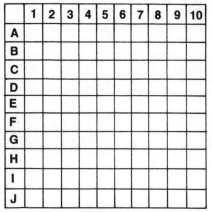

Enemy 2

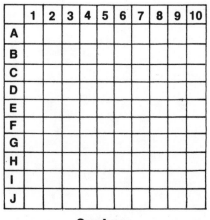

Our Army

WAR GAMING PRELIMINARY INSTRUCTION SHEET

The symbol of your team is a   square   circle   triangle

                                          □   O   Δ

Your team is to:

1. Design a national flag that incorporates this symbol;
2. Create a national anthem (something like a drinking song);
3. Establish nationalistic goals (such as revenge for real or imagined transgressions of one or more members of other teams against members of your team, a desire for more territory, etc.).

You are to assume that conflict is inevitable. Problems can be solved only by force of arms. Do your best to justify your conflict with the other teams. You will have fifteen minutes to complete these tasks.

WAR GAMING CONFLICT INSTRUCTION SHEET

The conflict will begin when one team calls out its first three shots at the end of the strategy session. After that, the play will rotate clockwise, as follows:

1. The team captain will call out three shots as a military order by naming the enemy (enemy team 1 or 2) and then the three grid spaces at which it will fire (letter-number, letter-number, letter-number) on the enemy's War Gaming Grid Map. Any order called out must be followed, even if it is redundant. No order can be retracted. Only the team captain may call out orders.
2. If the designated enemy has a tank, artillery battery, or infantry unit in a grid square named, it must assume a direct hit on that piece of equipment or unit and must mark out that portion of the piece or unit on the team's War Gaming Grid Map. The attacked team then calls out a damage report, saying "hit" or "miss" and naming only the letter and number of the occupied grid square that was hit but not identifying "what" was hit. (All hits and misses are subject to verification by the facilitator.)
3. All teams keep a record of shots fired (hits, H, and misses, M) by recording the appropriate letter on their grid map for each team.
4. Only thirty seconds is allowed between the completion of the damage report and the next team's calling of firing orders. Any shots not called in thirty seconds are declared "misfires," and the play advances to the next team.

It is important that each team plan its firing strategy *before* the commencement of hostilities.

265. MONETARY INVESTMENT: NEGOTIATION

Goals

I. To provide insight into the dynamics of negotiation processes: strategy, constituent pressure, consensus, and mediation.

II. To simulate a collective-bargaining experience.

III. To explore the behavior of participants in a bargaining situation.

Group Size

Twelve or more members.

Time Required

One and one-half to two hours.

Materials

I. Money in bills of any denomination.

II. Blank paper and a pencil for each participant.

Physical Setting

Three rooms, two for private caucuses and one to serve as a common meeting room, each with tables and chairs.

Process

I. The facilitator divides the participants into Labor, Management, and Neutral teams. (This may be done at random or members may choose which group they wish to join. The Labor and Management teams can be of equal numbers, or Labor can be larger to simulate real conditions. Only two or three members are needed on the Neutral team.)

II. The facilitator takes the Labor group aside and collects an equal amount of money ($1 to $3) from each member (amount X), then does the same thing with the Management group (amount Y). The facilitator decides how much to collect from each group and instructs each group not to reveal the amount collected. The Neutral group members are not told either amount.

III. The facilitator adds money ($11 to $25) (amount Z) to amounts X and Y and announces the total of X, Y, and Z to all groups. (Each group knows only its own contribution and the total; the Neutral group knows only the total.)

IV. The facilitator distributes paper and pencils to all participants. He tells them that the issue to be discussed is distribution of the money between the Labor and Management teams. These two teams are instructed to go to separate rooms and organize for a negotiation session to be held in fifteen minutes to establish ground rules.

V. The facilitator instructs the members of the Neutral group to prepare a brief presentation of what they offer, e.g., mediation, conciliation, go-between services, binding final-offer arbitration, arbitration with power to determine the settlement figure, or a hearing. The facilitator may discuss possible services with them. He tells them that they are to charge a set fee for their mediation and arbitration services. If their services are not hired, they are merely to observe the negotiation sessions.

VI. All members reassemble, and the Neutral group gives its presentation.

VII. The facilitator announces that after the first hour has passed, an amount of money (amount W) will be taken from the total every ten minutes (to simulate a no-contract, no-work strike situation) until a settlement is reached and that either team may have any amount deducted from the total as requested by an authorized agent (to simulate a lockout, if requested by management, or strike, if requested by labor). The facilitator keeps any money removed from the total.

VIII. Negotiation sessions begin and continue until a settlement has been reached about the distribution of the funds. The funds are then distributed as agreed.

IX. The facilitator leads a discussion of the feelings of the participants and the learnings that occurred. Some or all of the following questions may be used:

1. What were the reactions of the participants to the final settlement? How was it reached?
2. What were the reactions if money was deducted from the total? How did this affect the negotiation process?
3. What were the reactions to the negotiator on the part of each team?
4. What behaviors seemed to produce the best results for the bargaining parties involved? What other strategies might have been used?
5. What assumptions did the teams make about themselves and each other? How did this affect the bargaining position and strategy?
6. What principles (characteristics) are essential to the position of negotiator?

7. How would you modify these learnings when doing other types of negotiation?

Variations

I. The Neutral group members can be briefed on what to look for and can serve as discussion leaders.

II. If the group is large, some members can be briefed by the facilitator and act as silent observers at strategy sessions.

III. A different member of the Neutral group can serve at each session.

IV. The facilitator can give a lecturette on negotiation as part of step IV, or the Neutral group can expand its presentation.

V. Teams can reverse roles, if time permits, to gain a broader perspective.

Similar Structured Experiences: *Vol. II:* Structured Experience **36;** *Vol. III:* **61, 62, 68;** *'72 Annual:* **78, 83;** *'75 Annual:* **144, 145, 147;** *'77 Annual:* **186, 189;** *Vol. VI:* **217;** *'78 Annual:* **231;** *Vol. VII:* **263.**
Suggested Instrument: *'78 Annual:* "Mach V Attitude Inventory."
Lecturette Sources: *'73 Annual:* "Win/Lose Situations," "Confrontation: Types, Conditions, and Outcomes"; *'74 Annual:* "Conflict-Resolution Strategies"; *'76 Annual:* "Power"; *'77 Annual:* "Constructive Conflict in Discussion: Learning to Manage Disagreements Effectively," "Handling Group and Organizational Conflict."

Notes on the Use of "Monetary Investment":

Submitted by Tom Armor. A previous version of this structured experience appeared as "A Real Negotiation Exercise" in the *Journal of Collective Negotiations*, 1977, 6(2), 177-180.

266. POWER PERSONALITIES: AN OD ROLE PLAY

Goals

    I. To provide an opportunity to practice various power styles and behaviors.

    II. To learn which power-seeking tactics and bases of power are effective or ineffective in a problem-solving situation.

    III. To examine individual perceptions of and reactions to various power strategies.

Group Size

Four or five groups of seven or eight members each.

Time Required

Approximately one and one-half to two hours.

Materials

    I. A name tag bearing one of the seven Power Personalities roles for each role player in each group.

    II. A copy of the Power Personalities Background and Instruction Sheet for each role player from each group and for each observer.

    III. One copy of a different Power Personalities Role-Description Sheet for each of the seven role players from each group.

    IV. A copy of the Power Personalities Questionnaire Sheet for each participant.

    V. Blank paper and a pencil for each role player and each observer.

    VI. Newsprint and a felt-tipped marker for each group.

Physical Setting

A room large enough to accommodate a large table with chairs around it for each group, with enough room between the groupings to allow each group to role play independently.

Process

I. The facilitator gives a lecturette on the six bases of power[1]: reward, coercive, legitimate, expert, information, and referent.

II. The facilitator arranges the name tags face down in groups of seven, one group for each power personality, and has each member select a tag, sight unseen, and put it on. The facilitator divides the participants into groups of seven members each, with one of each of the seven Power Personalities in each group. Additional members serve as observers, balanced among the groups.

III. The facilitator distributes a copy of the Power Personalities Background and Instruction Sheet and the appropriate Power Personalities Role-Description Sheet to each role player in each group. Each observer receives a copy of the Power Personalities Background and Instruction Sheet. Each participant also receives blank paper and a pencil. The facilitator tells the participants that they have ten minutes in which to read their roles and instructions.

IV. The participants in each group are instructed to select chairs around their group's table.

V. The facilitator briefly describes the task and tells the participants that they have forty-five minutes in which to conduct the role play; he then turns the meeting over to the president in each group and the role play begins.

VI. The facilitator gives a ten-minute warning signal to ensure time for the secret ballots. At the end of the forty-five-minute period, he calls time to end the meeting.

VII. The facilitator distributes copies of the Power Personalities Questionnaire Sheet—to be completed by each participant—which will serve as the basis for subsequent discussion. (Fifteen minutes.) The results of the responses to the questionnaire are summarized within each group and displayed on newsprint.

---

[1]As proposed by French, J. R. P., Jr., & Raven, B., "The Bases of Social Power," in D. Cartwright (Ed.), *Studies in Social Power*, Ann Arbor: University of Michigan Press, 1959; Raven, B., "Social Influence and Power," in I. Steiner & M. Fishbein (Eds.), *Current Studies in Social Psychology*, New York: Holt, Rinehart and Winston, 1965; and Raven, B., & Kruglanski, A., "Conflict and Power," in P. Swingle (Ed.), *The Structure of Conflict*, New York: Academic Press, 1970.

VIII. The facilitator leads a discussion of the experience, including feelings of role players about themselves and each other during the activity, verbal and nonverbal behaviors that contributed to power strategies, reports from observers, bases of power that seem most influential in an organizational environment, learnings or general principles that emerged, and application to real-life situations.

Variations

I. The group can reach a decision verbally rather than by secret ballot.

II. Roles can be switched halfway through the role play.

III. Observers can serve as consultants in the decision-making process.

IV. New information ("news releases") can be introduced by the facilitator.

Similar Structured Experiences: *Vol. II:* Structured Experience **41**; *Vol. III:* **59**; *Vol. IV:* **108**; *'75 Annual:* **144**; *Vol. V:* **167**; *'77 Annual:* **186, 192, 195**; *Vol. VI:* **214**.

Suggested Instruments: *'78 Annual:* "Mach V Attitude Inventory"; *'79 Annual:* "Power and OD Intervention Analysis (PODIA)."

Lecturette Source: *'76 Annual:* "Power."

Notes on the Use of "Power Personalities":

Submitted by Laura A. Jean, Jeffrey R. Pilgrim, Gary N. Powell, Deborah K. Stoltz, and Olivia S. White.

POWER PERSONALITIES BACKGROUND AND INSTRUCTION SHEET

Background

The National Electronics Company is the third largest producer of electronic components, calculators, watches, and television video games in the United States. This industry is "labor intensive," that is, many persons are involved in assembling the products. NEC has approximately 23,000 employees and is organized as follows:

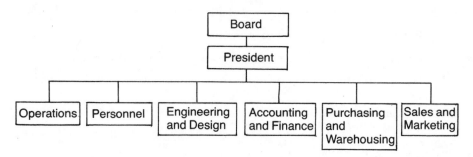

Almost all hourly employees at NEC are members of one union. Company sales last year totaled $300 million.

NEC corporate headquarters currently consist of several floors of a luxurious office building in midtown Manhattan. Manufacturing operations are located on Long Island and consist of several small, outdated plants.

The company is currently experiencing strong competition from foreign firms that have been able to hold their operating expenses down by employing cheap, nonunion labor. Further, there is a need for additional modernized manufacturing space in the next couple of years to accommodate new product lines and increased production of current products.

For several months a special task force commissioned by the chairman of the board and chaired by the manager of operations has been working to develop a proposal to meet the competition as well as future space requirements. Their proposal calls for relocation of the entire firm, its manufacturing and corporate divisions, to an industrial-park area in a Southeastern state. In this proposed location, manufacturing space can be doubled for the same cost as the current space, and there is an abundance of unskilled labor.

The president of NEC has called a meeting of the top-management team to decide whether or not the firm should relocate as proposed by the task force. A decision by the end of the meeting is necessary so that the president can present the management recommendations to the board the following morning. Because of special arrangements with respect to purchase of the land, the firm must move as a whole or not at all.

Instructions

1. You and the other members of the management team are to present and discuss your positions regarding the relocation outlined above and, by the end of the meeting, are to accept or reject the task force's proposal. The management team is composed of:

   President
   Manager of Operations
   Manager of Personnel
   Manager of Engineering and Design
   Manager of Accounting and Finance
   Manager of Purchasing and Warehousing
   Manager of Sales and Marketing.

   Each Power Personality Role-Description Sheet outlines an initial position or opinion as to the advisability of the move: for, against, neutral. This is only a *suggested* position. You should feel free to switch sides and/or be influenced by the arguments of the other players within the limits of your role. Any members without roles to play will act as observers.

2. Throughout the role play, you are to assume and display the power-personality characteristics outlined in your role description. Level of commitment to the goals of the firm, as opposed to personal goals, will be left up to the individual role players.

3. A secret-ballot vote will be taken by the president at the end of the meeting, and the results will be announced. The relocation decision will be determined by majority rule.

4. At the conclusion of the activity, you will be asked to complete a questionnaire based on your experience in the role play.

POWER PERSONALITIES ROLE-DESCRIPTION SHEET

President

Your position: Against the move

You have been with the National Electronics Company since its founding and have worked your way up from your original job in operations. During the ten years that you have been president, you have been committed to the success of the firm, have carried it through the lean years, and have contributed enormous energy toward making the firm the success it is today. You understand the possibilities for expansion and growth that the move to the Southern location could offer the firm. However, you are getting older and definitely feel reluctant to undertake the relocation of your family, the sale of your beautiful home, and the separation from friends that the move would require. Also, an important consideration is that you would be losing proximity to your Wall Street contacts— important to your private investments. Although you have not announced it yet, you intend to retire in a couple of years, and the company's move could force you to retire before you had intended.

You know that the manager of accounting and finance is strongly in favor of the move. However, you are wary of his evidence, since in the past he has overstated the benefits and understated the costs of capital projects.

Your power personality

Past experience has shown you that your positional power and the weight of your seniority can be used effectively to influence and control others. Your long years of experience make you a credible authority on a variety of matters. You know the workings of the firm inside and out.

You use occasional unpredictability as your ace in the hole, catching others off guard by either saying or doing what they least expect. You tend to be calm and soft spoken most of the time but have found that occasional outbursts of simulated anger (and a penchant for spicy language) can often shock people into compliance.

POWER PERSONALITIES ROLE-DESCRIPTION SHEET

Manager of Operations

Your position: For the move

The relocation plan is your brainchild. You feel strongly that the move will be good for the National Electronics Company financially, and operations can only be expanded if some kind of move is made soon. You feel that you are heir apparent to the presidency of the firm, and you would like to start influencing the firm's future in the most obvious way possible: by ushering in a new era of growth for the company. The move is bound to force some early retirements and resignations among management personnel who want to remain in the New York area. You feel that this will revitalize the organization, especially with some of the go-getter replacements you have in mind.

Your power personality

You have found that few opponents can withstand the force and high-energy level of your arguments. You are not afraid to shout someone down or to interrupt at strategic points in the discussion. In fact, you are rather rude. You are not above instilling a little fear in others by reminding them that you control the most important part of the firm: its manufacturing operations.

You are quick to pick out a person's weakness and capitalize on it. Emotional arguments or personal considerations are very easy to attack. You single-mindedly intend to get your way.

POWER PERSONALITIES ROLE-DESCRIPTION SHEET

Manager of Personnel

Your position: For the move

You are in favor of the move since there will be a wealth of semiskilled and trainable people in the area surrounding the new plant site. You know that restaffing will be an enormous job, but this very requirement could be an opportunity for you to increase your somewhat tentative power position in the firm by demanding that your department's staff be increased to handle the hiring job ahead. Also, you perceive that many of the managers—especially the operations manager, who helped you get your job a few years ago—are in favor of the move. You feel that you should return the favor and support their position.

Your power personality

From past experience you have found that being on the winning side has given you the prestige of being a "winner." You have become adept at spotting the "power person" in most group situations. By exhibiting compliant behavior and vocal support of that person's ideas and proposals, you will be seen as part of the inner power circle. Power does rub off. Also, you like to make sure that people are aware of your efforts on their behalf so that the favor will be returned.

POWER PERSONALITIES ROLE-DESCRIPTION SHEET

Manager of Engineering and Design

Your position: Against the move

Traditionally, one of the great advantages for your department is that the New York City area provides a wealth of technical talent, both for engineering and design positions within the firm and for a wide selection of outside consultants and research facilities. You are certain that a move by the company will cause attrition of some of your best people. Also, you foresee greatly increased research costs because of lack of access to both talent and product-development facilities. It is your view that the high quality of your engineering and design operation holds the key to meeting future competition effectively. A move to the new Southern location may cause the company to lose this present competitive edge. Finally, the move will afford operations additional manufacturing space (not surprising since the relocation is the operations manager's brainchild), with *no* increase in laboratory space.

Your power personality

You try to appear calm, cool, and level-headed. One way to get your point across in a debate is to repeat your statement of position over and over, never raising your voice, and looking your opponent straight in the eye. You counter the arguments of others by an appeal to logic: the most rational alternative must be the best one. You do not attack your opponents directly, but, rather, attack the logic of their arguments by questioning their research methods and basic assumptions. You are open minded to the extent that a more logical solution than your own may sway you.

POWER PERSONALITIES ROLE-DESCRIPTION SHEET

Manager of Accounting and Finance

Your position: For the move

You are in favor of the move because of the positive effect it will have on the bottom line. Building the needed manufacturing space in the new Southern location will be much less expensive than trying to expand here in New York City—even if you could find the land available. Net operating income has increased enormously in the past few years, but lack of expansion space will put a ceiling on earnings within a very short time. The strength of the company's financial position and the growth potential of the relocation would really be a boost to the company's stock sales. In addition, investment tax credits, lower energy costs, lower labor costs, and lower state taxes in the Southern location make the move very sensible.

Your power personality

You are very careful to have the hard facts about any question before you enter the discussion. You are willing and able to research these facts to enable you to use them to counter emotional arguments. You have a great deal of financial information at your disposal. As almost every activity in the company affects the bottom line, your auditors' examination of every department has given you a great deal of information about the efficiency of these departments as well as an awareness of a number of skeletons in various closets.

You are soft-spoken, which requires others to listen carefully when you speak. Your power tactic consists largely of strategic use of information, both financial and your own personal experience. Typically, you will let an opponent expound his views, then submit your information, pointing out that his argument is based on opinion while yours is based on hard facts.

POWER PERSONALITIES ROLE-DESCRIPTION SHEET

Manager of Purchasing and Warehousing

Your position: Against the move

You have been with the National Electronics Company for twenty-five years and are reluctant to leave the New York area, where you have a family and social ties. You think that many others in the company feel the same way you do about leaving New York. With only a few years left until retirement, you do not want to make any drastic changes in your life.

In terms of logistics, the new Southern location lacks easy access and efficient facilities for shipping your products and for receiving raw materials. You think that these increased transportation costs are a legitimate argument against moving to the new location.

Your power personality

You are personally very suspicious of change. You like the feeling of power you get by—at least initially—saying "no" to any proposal that involves making changes in the traditional way of doing things, regardless of well-supported arguments for the change. You have found that intransigence on your part can produce the desired effect of stopping the proceedings and can cause efforts on the part of others to placate you. When others demand reasons for your refusal, you know you can always blow up any small legitimate objection to defend your position. You are not afraid to let your tone of voice and bodily posture convey that you think people are picking on you unduly. You have often found that if you complain long enough and persistently enough, you will get your way.

POWER PERSONALITIES ROLE-DESCRIPTION SHEET

Manager of Sales and Marketing

Your position: Neutral

You can say with pride that the fact that the firm can even consider the proposed expansion move is a direct result of the jump in revenue from increased sales since you took over as manager of sales and marketing three years ago. Your innovative team-marketing and sales approach has been successful in selling the firm's products, by emphasizing their high quality of workmanship and providing customers with engineering and design services as part of the package when they buy electronic components.

Moving to the South would open up new geographical markets that have been neglected in the past. You personally would look forward to moving away from New York City. However, you are afraid that the proposed relocation of the firm's headquarters would mean the loss of some of your best sales people. Also, you would sorely miss the access to skilled advertising people and to the media that New York City provides. Move or no move, you are confident that your high sales accomplishments will continue.

Your power personality

You enjoy using your skills as a conciliator—a mediator of different points of view—to get questions settled quickly. You have confidence that your cheerful, humorous, positive, "let's get things settled to everyone's advantage" approach will gain you prestige as the one who engineered the solution to the problem. Periodically during the meeting, you take it upon yourself to summarize the various positions expressed by the members of the management team and to keep the discussion on track.

POWER PERSONALITIES QUESTIONNAIRE SHEET

Instructions

1. On the following Power Scale, circle the number that best represents your perception of the power that each of the company officers had in this meeting. At the side of each scale, indicate the basis of each officer's power, i.e.:

   - expert (E);
   - legitimate (L);
   - coercive (C);
   - reward (R);
   - referent (REF);
   - information (I);
   - or none (N).

Power Scale	*Power Base*

President

No 1 2 3 4 5 6 7 8 9 10 Very
Power   Powerful   _____

Manager of Operations

No 1 2 3 4 5 6 7 8 9 10 Very
Power   Powerful   _____

Manager of Personnel

No 1 2 3 4 5 6 7 8 9 10 Very
Power   Powerful   _____

Manager of Engineering and Design

No 1 2 3 4 5 6 7 8 9 10 Very
Power   Powerful   _____

Manager of Accounting and Finance

No 1 2 3 4 5 6 7 8 9 10 Very
Power   Powerful   _____

Manager of Purchasing and Warehousing

No 1 2 3 4 5 6 7 8 9 10 Very
Power   Powerful   _____

Manager of Sales and Marketing

No <u>1 2 3 4 5 6 7 8 9 10</u> Very
Power   Powerful   _____

2. In the space below, draw an organization chart for the National Electronics
   Company. Show where the *real* power and influence lie by varying the size of
   the boxes on the chart and drawing lines between them to depict the informal
   channels of power or powerful subgroups. You may refer to the Power Personalities Background and Instruction Sheet as you perform this task.

267. WHOM TO CHOOSE: VALUES AND GROUP DECISION MAKING

Goals

    I. To examine and make choices concerning one's own values.

    II. To assess the degree to which members of a group have common values and the impact of this on group decision making.

    III. To observe problem-solving strategies in groups.

Group Size

Any number of groups of five to seven members each.

Time Required

Forty-five minutes to one hour.

Materials

    I. A copy of the Whom to Choose Nominees Sheet for each participant.

    II. A copy of one of the three Whom to Choose Situation Description Sheets for each participant.

    III. Newsprint and a felt-tipped marker for each group.

Physical Setting

A room large enough to accommodate a circle of chairs for each group and to allow for a general group discussion.

Process

    I. The facilitator forms groups by any appropriate method. He describes the goals of the activity. He explains that it is much more difficult to make choices based on values than on facts, but that we often make unconscious "value" decisions, and that part of self-growth can include understanding one's own value system in order to make more intelligent or appropriate choices.

II. The facilitator distributes a copy of the Whom to Choose Nominees Sheet and a copy of one of the Whom to Choose Situation Description Sheets to each participant (all members of a group receive the same situation sheet, but different groups may work on different situations). The facilitator announces that individuals will have five minutes to make personal choices and that each group will then have thirty minutes to make its selection and post it on newsprint.

III. When the groups have completed the activity, the total group is assembled, and the facilitator leads a discussion of the results of the groups' deliberations, how different situations yielded different preferences, how these compared with individual decisions, the results of any conflict between the two, the feelings of the members about the activity, how personal values affected the problem-solving strategies and the decision-making process, and how this applies to other situations in which values may be important to a decision.

Variations

I. Each group can make its final choices and develop a strategy for debating them. The facilitator then chooses two or three groups that have made very different choices. These groups present their arguments to the total group, after which the nondebating participants vote for the group they agree with most. A discussion of the effects of persuasion follows.

II. Instead of choosing six people from the sheet of nominees, participants can rank order each of the twenty-four names, using "1" as the first choice and "24" as the last, or pick the top three and bottom three from the list of twenty-four.

III. Names of persons who are prominent in the local community, in the recent news, or in other fields can be used.

Similar Structured Experiences: *Vol. I:* Structured Experiences **11, 15;** *Vol. II:* **30;** *Vol. III:* **69;** *'72 Annual:* **77;** *'73 Annual:* **94;** *Vol. IV:* **113, 115;** *'74 Annual:* **127, 134, 135;** *Vol. V:* **157;** *'78 Annual:* **223;** *'79 Annual:* **235;** *Vol. VII:* **248.**

Lecturette Sources: *'73 Annual:* "Synergy and Consensus-Seeking," "Some Implications of Value Clarification for Organization Development"; *'78 Annual:* "Utilizing Human Resources: Individual Versus Group Problem Solving and Decision Making."

Submitted by Charles L. Eveland and Dorothy M. Hai.

Notes on the Use of "Whom to Choose":

WHOM TO CHOOSE NOMINEES SHEET

Woody Allen
Neil Armstrong
Melvin Belli
Julian Bond
Joyce Brothers
Anita Bryant
William F. Buckley
Jacques Cousteau
Walter Cronkite
Chris Everts
John Kenneth Galbraith
Billy Graham

Alex Haley
Jesse Jackson
Bruce Jenner
Edward Kennedy
Coretta King
Claire Booth Luce
Liza Minnelli
Walter Mondale
Rudolph Nureyev
Robert Redford
Jonas Salk
Gloria Steinem

WHOM TO CHOOSE SITUATION DESCRIPTION SHEET

Kidney Transplant

Since kidney dialysis has become very rare, people who have nonfunctioning kidneys all want transplants. Those who cannot receive these transplants will probably die in one or two years. Unfortunately, there are many more applicants than there are available kidneys.

Scandinavian Medical Center in Houston, Texas, has become renowned for its kidney transplants. A committee of doctors screens all applicants to see who would physically benefit most from a kidney transplant. For instance, a person with chronic emphysema or some other debilitating disease might not recover well from the operation.

You are on the hospital's final screening committee. All the applicants on your list have been determined to benefit equally from the transplant. Assume they will all match the donors. Now it is up to you to make a choice about which *six* people will receive kidneys this year. Rank order the six by importance, because it may be that only four or five kidneys will be available. In addition, rank order two alternatives, since there might be as many as eight kidneys available for transplants.

You will then share your choices with your group, and it will make a final decision.

WHOM TO CHOOSE SITUATION DESCRIPTION SHEET

Lifeboat

The S.S. Titanic II has just hit an iceberg and will sink in one hour. All lifeboats are assigned except one. For this last lifeboat you must select six people from the list of twenty-four. Remember, these six people will be the only survivors of the group of twenty-four.

After that is done, your next task is the allocation of resources. The lifeboat contains enough food and water for seven days. Assume a rescue will not occur before seven days and may take as many as fourteen. If this is so, food must be severely rationed. You must decide what to do in case a fourteen-day lifeboat stay is required:

1. Reduce everyone's food by one-half.
2. Reduce some of the group (of six) members' food and not others, so that those with full allocations of food have a greater chance to make it through the fourteen days.

You will then share your choices with your group, and it will make a final decision.

WHOM TO CHOOSE SITUATION DESCRIPTION SHEET

Spaceship

The Spaceship Foundation is preparing to send a craft on a journey through our galaxy. It will contain information on the earth's cultures, history, and notable people.

You must choose six notable people (from the list of twenty-four) whose biographies will be included with the Foundation's material. This material is intended to be intercepted by extraterrestrial beings and will serve as the basis for the impressions they form of the United States and of Earth in general.

You will then share your choices with your group, and it will make a final decision.

268. SEXUAL VALUES IN ORGANIZATIONS: AN OD ROLE PLAY

Goals

I. To identify a range of personal, ethical, professional, and organizational considerations related to sexual relationships that occur between members of an organization.

II. To determine the effect of such relationships on individual as well as organizational effectiveness.

Group Size

A maximum of twenty members, preferably persons who have some acquaintance with one another. (A balance of males and females is desirable.)

Time Required

Three hours.

Materials

I. Two copies of the Sexual Values in Organizations Role-Play Sheet to be distributed to two role players (preferably prior to the session).

II. A copy of the Sexual Values in Organizations Questionnaire for each participant.

Physical Setting

A room in which participants can sit comfortably in a circle. An additional, small room is desirable, but not necessary.

Process

I. The facilitator selects two members, preferably a male and a female, to conduct the role play. He gives them each a copy of the Sexual Values in Organizations Role-Play Sheet and directs them to a separate room or a far corner of the room to prepare their roles.[1]

---

[1] It is most effective if the role players can be given sufficient time to prepare the role play before the group session.

II. The facilitator discusses the goals and design of the experience with the remainder of the group.

III. The Sexual Values in Organizations Questionnaire is distributed to each participant. Participants are told to complete it, then to turn it over and put it aside until the second half of the session. (Ten minutes.)

IV. The facilitator calls in the two role players and then introduces the first role play to the entire group, giving a description of the setting and a brief outline of the scene. The role play is then enacted by the two group members who have prepared for it. (Fifteen minutes.) The second and third role plays are introduced and conducted, in turn.

V. The facilitator leads a discussion in which the group members explore:
   1. Their reactions to the role play.
   2. Personal related experiences in organizations (as participants or observers).
   3. Observations about the effect of intimate sexual relationships on organizational behavior and on the effectiveness of people in organizations.
   (One-half hour.)

VI. The group is divided into dyads (preferably male-female); dyads are directed to discuss their responses to the Sexual Values in Organizations Questionnaire. (Ten minutes.)

VII. When the dyads have discussed their questions, the total group is reassembled, and the members report on their discussions. The facilitator may then ask the following questions:
   1. What are the costs, benefits, and implications of sexual relationships in organizations for individuals and for the organization?
   2. In our dealings with people, do we give preference to those who are most sexually attractive to us?
   3. What is meant by the term "professional behavior?"
   4. What are the power factors involved in the seduction of employees by clients, bosses by subordinates, or instructors by students, and vice versa?
   5. How do we determine which behavior should be enforced in the organizational context? According to whose values? How should that behavior be enforced?
   6. By enforcing certain values and behavior, do we limit *ourselves* as well as others? Are we willing to do that?
   7. How does sexual stereotyping relate to intimate relationships in organizations?
   8. How are sexual and sex-role binds played out in the organization?
   9. How do our own personal values relate to our actual behavior? What is

the relationship of those values to our profession and sense of professionalism?

(Approximately twenty minutes.)

Variations

I. The Sexual Values in Organizations Questionnaire can be omitted and the discussion focused on the role play that occurred.

II. The discussion questions can be omitted, and the dyads can focus on the Sexual Values in Organizations Questionnaire.

III. The role play can be omitted and the discussion focused on exploring issues contained in the Sexual Values in Organizations Questionnaire.

IV. Males and females can be separated into groups of the same sex to discuss the questionnaire.

V. The role players can be two individuals of the same sex. In this case, participants usually focus more on homosexuality and related dynamics and less on organizational behavior. The goals of the activity are then changed to reflect more appropriately the focus on feelings, attitudes, and experiences related to homosexuality.

Similar Structured Experiences: *'73 Annual:* Structured Experiences **94, 95;** *'76 Annual:* **184;** *Vol. VI:* **215;** *'78 Annual:* **226;** *Vol. VII:* **248, 249, 258.**

Suggested Instruments: *'73 Annual:* "Sex-Role Stereotyping Rating Scale"; *'77 Annual:* "Bem Sex-Role Inventory (BSRI)"; *'79 Annual:* "Women as Managers Scale (WAMS)."

Lecturette Sources: *'73 Annual:* "Some Implications of Value Clarification for Organization Development"; *'77 Annual:* "Androgyny," "Organizational Norms."

Notes on the Use of "Sexual Values in Organizations":

Submitted by Peggy Morrison. (The questionnaire was developed in collaboration with Richard DeGraw.)

SEXUAL VALUES IN ORGANIZATIONS ROLE-PLAY SHEET

The goals of this experience are to identify a range of personal, ethical, professional, and organizational considerations related to sexual relationships that occur between members of an organization and to determine the effect of such relationships on individual as well as organizational effectiveness.

You are one of two volunteers selected to create roles to reflect each of the three scenarios below. Each scenario should take no more than five minutes. You can proceed immediately from Scene 1 to Scene 2 to Scene 3 with a brief pause between them, or can introduce them as "Scene 1," "Scene 2," and "Scene 3."

You and your fellow role player will develop these scenes as you wish in terms of (a) organizational roles played and (b) the dynamics of each scenario, i.e., what positive and negative aspects of the relationship you choose to act out. Each scenario is in an organizational setting.

Scene 1: Two people in an organization who have for some time had a strong sexual attraction for each other are deciding to act on their sexual feelings and to expand their relationship to be more sexually intimate.

Scene 2: The same people, several months into the relationship, are in their organizational roles, and the scene reflects the effects that the relationship is having both on the individuals and their performances in the organization.

Scene 3: Following the breakup of the relationship of the two individuals, they are shown in the organizational setting, and the scene reflects what effects the termination of their intimate relationship is having on the individuals, their work in the organization, and the organization itself.

SEXUAL VALUES IN ORGANIZATIONS QUESTIONNAIRE

Instructions: This is a survey of your opinions concerning sexuality in work situations. In responding to the following items, check *yes* if you believe a statement to be *true most of the time* and *no* if you believe the statement to be *false most of the time*.

Yes   No

1. Extramarital sex is healthy.

2. Sexual relations foster better communication between the persons involved.

3. A person's personal life is his or her own business.

4. Premarital sex is damaging to the persons involved.

5. Extramarital sex is damaging to the persons involved.

6. The attitude of other workers would remain the same toward me if I were having sexual relations with the supervisor and were promoted over six other candidates.

7. Married workers should be reprimanded for having sexual relations with other workers.

8. Unmarried workers should be reprimanded for having sexual relations with other workers.

9. My opinion of my supervisor would be unchanged if I learned that he or she was homosexual.

10. Sexual intimacy among co-workers creates a more harmonious office environment.

11. It is perfectly acceptable for professional helping persons to have sexual relations with individuals whom they are helping.

12. I believe that it is all right to dress seductively at work to attract the attention of members of the opposite sex.

13. An administrator should be unconcerned with an employee's sexual habits.

14. I could work just as well with my supervisor after he or she ended a sexual affair with me.

15. Homosexuals should be denied the opportunity to work directly with people.

16. If I ended an affair with a co-worker, I believe that he or she would continue to treat me the way he or she was treating me during our affair.

17. I would agree to sexual relations with my supervisor if he or she promised me better pay if I cooperated.

18. Sexual relations among co-workers affect the workings of the office.

CONTRIBUTORS

Donald Anderson, Ed.D.
Coordinator, Counseling Services
Office of Student Development
Virginia Western Community College
3095 Colonial Avenue, S.W.
Roanoke, Virginia 24015
(703) 982-7237

Thomas H. Armor, Ph.D.
Consultant
4448 Wahinekoa Place
Honolulu, Hawaii 96821
(808) 737-3894

Dwight Bechtel
Associate Director
General Management Institute
Atlanta Regional Training Center
U.S. Civil Service Commission
1340 Spring Street
Atlanta, Georgia 30309
(404) 881-3837

Kenneth M. Bond, Ph.D.
Associate Professor of Management
  and Associate Dean
College of Business Administration
Creighton University
2500 California
Omaha, Nebraska 68178
(402) 449-2853

Charles L. Eveland, Ph.D.
Professor and Director
Center for Health Services Administration
Arizona State University
Tempe, Arizona 85281
(602) 965-7778

Peter G. Gillan, Ph.D.
Instructor
Human Services
Jamestown Community College
Jamestown, New York 14701
(716) 665-5220

Melvin A. Goldstein, Ph.D.
Assistant Professor of Psychology
Department of Psychology
Illinois State University
Normal, Illinois 61761
(309) 438-8651

Dorothy M. Hai, Ed.D.
Assistant Professor
Center for Health Services Administration,
  and Research Associate
Bureau of Business and Economic Research
Arizona State University
Tempe, Arizona 85281
(602) 965-3961

Brian P. Holleran, Ph.D.
Associate Professor
Department of Speech Communication
  and Theatre
State University of New York
Oneonta, New York 13820
(607) 431-3402

Branton K. Holmberg, Ed.D.
President, Holmberg Associates
Management and Organization Development
  Consultants
910 Yew Street
Bellingham, Washington 98225
(206) 676-9970

John E. Hoover, Ph.D.
Psychologist
Center for Psychology and Counseling
4877 Chambliss Avenue
Knoxville, Tennessee 37919
(615) 588-1923

Laura A. Jean
Employee Relations Specialist
3301 Raleigh Street
Denver, Colorado 80212
(303) 433-3562

John E. Jones, Ph.D.
Vice President
University Associates, Inc.
7596 Eads Avenue
La Jolla, California 92037
(714) 454-8821

Don Keyworth, Ph.D.
Professor of Philosophy
Drake University
Des Moines, Iowa 50311
(515) 271-3735

Barry D. Leskin
Manager, Organization Development
Sun Company, Inc.
100 Matsonford Road
Radnor, Pennsylvania 19087
(215) 293-6319

Donald E. Miskiman
Psychologist
Kings Regional Health and
   Rehabilitation Center
P.O. Box 128
Waterville, Nova Scotia B0P 1VO,
   Canada
(902) 538-3103

Peggy Morrison, Ph.D.
Management Consultant,
Assistant Professor
Organizational Behavior
School of Social Work
Arizona State University
Tempe, Arizona 85281
(602) 965-3304

Daniel W. Mullene
Import Account Executive
Geo. S. Bush & Co., Inc.
259 Colman Building
Seattle, Washington 98104
(206) 623-2593

Jeffrey R. Pilgrim
Trust Officer
Colonial Bancorp, Inc.
81 West Main Street
Waterbury, Connecticut 06702
(203) 574-7655

Gary N. Powell, Ph.D.
Assistant Professor of Management
   and Administrative Sciences
School of Business Administration
University of Connecticut
Storrs, Connecticut 06268
(203) 486-3862

Jay Proescher
Organization Development Consultant
Phoenix Associates
4125 Taylor Avenue
Baltimore, Maryland 21236
(301) 665-6646

Richard Raine
Training Officer I
Management and Staff Development Section
State of California Employee
   Development Department
800 Capitol Mall — MIC 44
Sacramento, California 95814
(916) 445-0247

J. Malcolm Rigby
Pacific Consultants
P.O. Box 682
Kuala Belait
State of Brunei, Borneo

Allen J. Schuh, Ph.D.
Professor of Management Sciences
School of Business and Economics
California State University
Hayward, California 94542
(415) 881-3322

Bradford F. Spencer
President, Spencer and Associates, Inc.
632 30th Street, Suite 2
Manhattan Beach, California 90266
(213) 546-1795

Deborah K. Stoltz
Financial Analyst
Pratt and Whitney Aircraft
East Hartford, Connecticut 06108
(203) 565-6752

Paul S. Weikert, Ph.D.
Assistant Professor
Central Michigan University,
Director
Human Relations Consultants, Inc.
535 Haslett Road
Williamston, Michigan 48895
(517) 655-2060

Olivia S. White
Senior Managing Consultant
Connecticut General Life Insurance
   Company
Hartford, Connecticut 06152
(203) 243-8811

David E. Whiteside, Ph.D.
Marriage and Family Counselor
Yadkin County Mental Health Center
P.O. Box 818
Yadkinville, North Carolina 27055
(919) 679-8265

Jack N. Wismer, Ph.D.
Organization Communication Consultant
Wismer Research and Training Consultants
5440 Lake Shore Drive
Littleton, Colorado 80123
(303) 798-2211

STRUCTURED EXPERIENCE CATEGORIES